STEWARDSHIP:
THE PROVEN PATH

STEWARDSHIP:
THE PROVEN PATH

James Denver Klote

Library of Congress Control Number: 2006907255
ISBN: Hardcover   978-1-4257-2916-5
               Softcover   978-1-4257-2915-8

This book was printed in the United States of America.

To order additional copies of this book, contact:
James D. Klote & Associates, Inc.
1-800-360-2315
www.jdklote.com
orders@jdklote.com
35981

CONTENTS

To the One who makes living a life of Christian Stewardship meaningful.

And to my wonderful wife, Molly, who encouraged me and
helped me to organize and share my experiences.

ABOUT THE AUTHOR

How did you get involved in fund-raising consulting?

After I graduated from college, I took a position with the United Way in Columbus, Ohio. I found that I had a talent at rallying support for a cause and motivating people to accomplish a goal. After a few years with them, Ward, Dreshman and Reinhardt (WD&R), the country's oldest and most prestigious fund-raising consulting firm, recruited me. At twenty-six, I was the youngest consultant the firm had ever hired.

Is it true that you became president of WD&R when you were thirty-two?

It is true. It is also unbelievable to me, given the history of that company, established in 1890 and a founding tenant in the Empire State Building and then in Rockefeller Center. I think that WD&R appreciated my devotion. I was the consummate company man. I went anywhere I was sent, to any campaign, no questions asked, and I got results. After a few years of that, the executives also realized that I had a talent for selling the WD&R service, mostly because I believed so deeply in the Plan of Campaign, if executed properly.

Why did you leave this company to start your own business?

After several years as president, I was growing increasingly less comfortable with the corporate culture of the company. The company thought it had more value than the needs of the client, and I was not comfortable in that environment, especially given the nature of our work. I did not want to leave WD&R. I loved the history of the company. I especially loved looking through all of the old photos of the past consultants. I felt a real connection to those who had come before me in this field of work, so I asked for a change in the corporate culture. The senior leadership at the time was not willing to change. It was one of the hardest decisions of my life but, with the support of my family, I turned in my resignation and informed the board of directors that I was leaving to start my own firm.

What was the reaction?

The board members were surprised at first, because most knew of my deep commitment to the firm; however, many of them also were upset with the direction of WD&R. It was at my impetus that they began to take action. Within hours of my resignation, every member of the board faxed in a resignation and contacted me about joining my new firm. It was a real vindication that the board members wanted to serve the clients, just as I did. I welcomed all of them and worked very hard to sell services to get them all employed again.

Was the new firm an immediate success?

Far from it. Name recognition in this business is essential and I had just abandoned the most famous name in private U.S. fund raising. It has taken me several years to get our name associated with the excellent service we provide. The tide finally turned a few years ago when instead of making calls looking for business, my phone started ringing on a daily basis. Now, I am constantly looking for talented people who might enjoy this line of work so I can keep up with the demand for full-time service.

What does the future hold for you?

God willing, I will have many more years of serving church clients and helping them to achieve their vision for their congregations. I can't imagine a more rewarding career. I also see no way around continuing to grow the firm. The number of requests we get for service is increasing exponentially each year.

If someone wishes to inquire about your services or inquire more about a position in your firm after reading your book, what is the best way to contact you?

All of our information is on our web site at *www.jdklote.com*. I am always happy to share my insight into a fund-raising situation, so I would encourage people to contact me if they are interested in our services for a Capital Campaign or are looking for ways to improve their Annual Campaigns. Certainly, if this type of work appeals to the reader, I would encourage anyone to contact my office.

PREFACE

If you are considering a Capital Campaign,* this book is required reading. It will help you understand the complexities of a Capital Campaign, introduce you to issues surrounding the selection of a consulting firm, and give you insight into problems you cannot yet conceive. This book will show you the plan; but, just like a map, it cannot get you there. That requires proper implementation through experienced guidance. You only have one opportunity to conduct your campaign properly. Short cuts will never give you the results you need and can be a terrible mistake. Although this book contains detailed information that may lead some to think they can use it as a Plan of Campaign, that is not the intent. This is not a how-to manual for directing a Capital Campaign. The book is designed to describe how complex the issues related to conducting the campaign can be and why professional help is required to achieve success.

Why would I write a book on such a specialized topic and seemingly give away the secrets to true church fund-raising success? That is the question that my consultants and I have grappled with for years. Over time, we came to the consensus that this information needs to be shared. It is the Christian thing to do. Part of our mission is to educate. Unfortunately, churches seem to learn lessons the hard way; knowledge of campaigns seems to only pass through storytelling and folklore. It was clear that I had a duty to put something in writing to help churches make good decisions regarding fund raising.

As a consultant over the past two decades, I have embraced a Plan of Campaign through which any church can maximize its fund-raising potential. This plan was not designed overnight; it is the result of thousands of hours of fund-raising experience. The true stories I share throughout the book illustrate the lessons I have learned so that you do not have to learn them. I generalized the stories so that no particular person or church could be identified. The church in which the lesson was learned is not as important as the lesson itself. I don't intend to sound didactic or boastful; the stories

11

are just a reflection of my experience. I find the same types of problems in every church campaign, and I am fortunate to be able to draw on my experience to solve them. I have found that there is one way to conduct a Capital Campaign correctly; there are a million ways to mess it up.

As the largest full-time, resident-directed, Church Capital Campaign consulting firm in the country, we have had the opportunity to present our plan to numerous churches considering campaigns. These churches typically interview one or two part-time firms for the project in addition to us. Years ago, when I was not selected to conduct campaigns, I followed up to find out why. It was inevitably the cost of our service. For a short time, I considered offering less expensive, part-time service. I mentioned it to my wife one evening; she was surprised and told me that she didn't think I could do that. When I asked her why, she said that she knew that deep down I did not believe in that type of service and, ultimately, if I didn't do what I believed was right for these churches, I would be unhappy and my career would suffer. She convinced me that I needed to demonstrate to churches that the return on the investment of full-time, resident-directed fund raising was worth the investment. She was right (as she often is), and my firm continues to offer only full-time consulting service.

When I decided to name my company, I went back and forth about whether to use my own name or create a sterile corporate name. After much thought and prayer, I decided to use my name so that clients would know that I am involved and their success is of personal importance to me. As it turns out, I find that I am typically involved more than most part-time consultants, and my involvement is in addition to the consultant who is working on the campaign full time. Therefore, churches are in essence getting two consultants for the price of one.

I have stopped counting the number of churches that have contacted me to help them salvage a campaign after they tried to conduct it on their own or went forward with an inferior method to save a little money. Ultimately, it costs them more money. The concept of return on investment is now clear to them; however, often the damage is so severe that we cannot be of assistance other than to encourage them to allow a period of time to go by and then begin again, correctly. This waiting period can be years. I have also stopped counting the number of times pastors tell me that this practical approach to church stewardship and the proven ways to identify and recruit the right church leaders to ensure an effective and productive campaign experience should be taught in seminary. I hope this book will begin that education process.

The central theme to any Capital Campaign needs to be stewardship. Stewardship is more than just fund raising, it is a process of encouraging a renewed sense of commitment to the church. Most likely, you have not had to build the church in which you are worshipping. I challenge every campaign committee to imagine that if the church were not there, what it would cost to build. In most cases, you are merely renovating what others had to sacrifice to build. One pastor called the process of stewardship "standing on the shoulders of giants," and I think that sentiment captures the idea and imagination of the generational connection that churches want to engender in their congregations.

Thank you for taking the time to read this book; it was a labor of love for me. I so enjoy what I do that I do not consider it work; it is my calling. I am very blessed in so many areas of my life including my wife, Molly; my children, Philip, Andrew, and Meredith; my many campaign consultants; the bishops, pastors, rectors, church business administrators, and lay leaders who I now call friends; and the opportunity to be able to participate in the spiritual lives of so many churches.

Jim Klote

*The terms "Capital Campaign" and "Stewardship Campaign" will be used interchangeably throughout the book.

CHAPTER 1

Soul Searching

Who are you?

You likely are reading this book because you are involved in some aspect of stewardship or development. Whether you are a member of the clergy, a church business administrator, or a key lay leader, the lessons should serve as a help and guide.

Perhaps you have just arrived at a church and see such great untapped potential that you have a fire in your belly to make a difference for the Lord. Or perhaps you have been at the church for years and are tired, but deep down you know that you are not doing all that you could to advance Christ's church here on earth. Perhaps you believe you are not doing enough—or that you already do too much. You have already asked the same people over and over again to give of their time and talents and they have risen to the occasion, but why is it always the same few people? How do you begin to decide what to do, whether it's to encourage more ministries and programs or recruit the involvement of more church members? How do you know what the congregation wants or needs? This is the place to start. Begin to answer these questions.

What kind of a church are you?

Demographics:

What is the average age of the members of your congregation?

> In the United States, the average age of all citizens is thirty-five. The average age of a worshiper in any mainstream faith is fifty. In the United Methodist Church, the average age of members nationwide is sixty. Presbyterians are on average fifty-eight years old. Catholics and Episcopalians are roughly fifty-seven and fifty-eight respectively. *Compilation of 2005 statistical data from the internet*

What is your congregation's age trend? Does the number keep going up, or has it gone down? Is there a balanced flow of people of all ages? Can you account for any particular ministry in your church that might attract either elderly members or younger members? Do you want to change that demographic?

Location:

Are you in the city or are you a rural church? How do you fit in with your community and how do its members perceive you? Do you fill an essential/needed role in the community, such as offering a meeting room for the Boy Scouts or Alcoholics Anonymous? Is your church merely a structure, or does it add value to the community? Does it serve as a third place, in addition to home and work, for people to gather and fill their social needs?

Style:

What sort of a style does your church have? Is it pastoral or is it program based? Is it the same style as when you arrived or has the congregation changed? Have you personally changed?

Communication:

How well do your members know each other, especially if they do not attend the same service? Do you ever sponsor a congregationwide event, or are all interactions service specific? Do members volunteer for activities outside their service time? What do the members think of the church, and how do you know? When was your last congregational meeting, if ever, and who attended? Is the only time you hear from most members when something is wrong? Are you only hearing grievances and not dreams?

Stewardship:

I recently had lunch with a pastor and the president of a large seminary. We were discussing stewardship and the pastor said, "I don't know anything about the financial contributions people make to the church, because it could affect how I provide ministry to them." The president of the seminary said very bluntly, "What other areas of their lives do you ignore? If knowing their gifts affects your ministry, perhaps you shouldn't minister."

If you are the pastor, are you involved in the stewardship committee and the process to fund annual ministries? If not, why not? How is your annual stewardship campaign conducted? Is it publicized? When does it occur in the calendar year? Is it an afterthought around the Christmas holiday? Is it a form letter? What percentage of your congregation pledges? *On average nationwide, 50 percent of church members pledge annually.* Who is involved in the campaign? Is the pastor involved? Does he/she offer a sermon on stewardship? Is person-to-person visitation encouraged? Is there fellowship involved in the asking?

How do you educate the congregation on stewardship in the church? Is it the once-a-year sermon? Do you publish a budget? Does anyone read the budget other than to see the church staff salaries? Does the pastor shy away from the topic of finances? Are all families treated equally and respectfully when asked to contribute? Is the focus on equal sacrifice, not equal giving?

Ministries:

Are your programs alive and well or struggling? Do you have a vibrant music program? What about a music director on staff? Do you need one? How many choirs are there? Are the youth involved? What youth programs do you offer? Do you have a youth pastor or youth director? Do you need one? Do you have enough staff? Are you drowning in paperwork or appointments? Do you wish you were drowning in appointments, but no one is calling on you? Do you offer Sunday school, Bible study, or Bible camp in the summer? Are you able to accommodate all those who want to participate in your ministries, or are some left out due to space constraints, staffing issues, or lack of funding? Are you having a hard time filling your ministry opportunities due to poor facilities? Does your Annual Campaign fund the ministries that you currently support? If not, why not? Have you embarked on a ministry that is not favored by the congregation? Are you truly trying to do too much? Are the congregation members communicating with you through their wallets?

Facilities:

How old are your facilities? Are you prepared for a surprise repair? Would that push your already strained budget over the limit? What if the boiler exploded tomorrow? Would you have the reserves to repair it? What about the roof? Have you been maintaining your stained-glass windows, or are they in need of maintenance? When was the last renovation, if ever? Is the facility in disrepair, or is it a model for your community?

Is your church pleasing and welcoming, or merely functional and adequate? Is the parking adequate for all services, or just for the earliest service with the least attendance? Is the facility handicapped accessible? If you wanted to expand your space, could you? Are you landlocked, leaving you with the options of building vertically only? Do you need to acquire other property on which to expand?

Finances:

Three years ago, I met with the pastor of a United Methodist church to discuss a building campaign for a growing congregation. As part of the campaign, the pastor wanted to try to rid the church of approximately $250,000 of debt. The congregation dragged its feet and Feasibility Studies were not even conducted. Recently, the same pastor called me. The church was now in real crisis. It was in desperate need of the same new facilities, but now the debt was over $1.4 million. The campaign's focus was now debt reduction, which is not as glamorous as a building effort. Even though the congregation members raised four times their annual giving, all they could do was pay off the debt.

Are you in debt supporting your current ministries or making the mortgage payment? Do you have an endowment? Do you really want an endowment? Do you have any other assets?

An Episcopal church was left a sizable endowment by a member who had passed away. The church was thrilled. It served initially as a way to back small loans for the church that were then paid off quickly. The principal was never touched. Years went by and a new pastor came to the church. Many of the lay leadership changed positions, and few members really remembered who had given the endowment or why. As time passed, the church needed many things. The church committee considered the pros and cons of taking loans versus using the principal of the endowment versus conducting a fund-raising campaign to pay for needed repairs and missions. As everyone was almost in agreement that the principal of the endowment should be spent, a member of the congregation approached the pastor and asked why this course of action was being considered. The pastor told the man that this was an easier path than conducting a campaign; after all, the money was already there. The man said in protest, "Do you really think that this is why we were left this money? The endowment was left as a testament of his faith. If he knew it would end up being the cause of laziness among the next generation of supposedly faithful, I am certain he would not have left it." The pastor addressed the church council with these sentiments and the council decided to proceed with a Capital Campaign. The members worked diligently to achieve a major success, raising ten times their annual giving. Today, they still enjoy the security of their endowment and have a financial buffer for unforeseen events.

> Contrast that with a parish that hired a part-time, inexperienced consultant to run its building campaign. After almost a year of paying for the consultant's services, the church did not raise even one times annual giving. As the needs were quite urgent, the church council made the desperate decision to liquidate an endowment that had taken the church over fifty years to accumulate.

Now that you have read through that litany of questions and have been assessing your own situation, take a moment to imagine your vision for your church if money were no object. Imagine not only what you need, but also what you want.

Vision:

Do you need to change the type of church that you are? Have you become exclusive rather than inclusive for any number of reasons? Perhaps your congregation likes being the size it is and doesn't want to encourage growth. Is the church growing or dying? What would you do to the facilities? What is your ideal staff size? What about programs—would you cut some, add some? What if you could have an endowment? Do you have unmet ministry needs? Are those needs within the community, or can you contribute to a national need? Or are you looking to contribute to some international need?

> I recently attended a discernment program at a Catholic church and the priest from another parish, who was leading the retreat, had all of us write down the tangible things we wanted for the church, if money were no object. We all wrote down our dreams. He kept record of all the dreams on a large piece of butcher block paper in the front of the room. The priest then turned to us and said, "I have good news. There is not one thing on this list that you cannot have. All you have to do is either redirect current monies to these projects or encourage support for these new items."

This priest was absolutely right. There isn't anything you cannot do with the support of the congregation. Perhaps it is a matter of redirecting monies or encouraging inspirational giving from the congregation to support something new that the congregation in general supports. This book is designed to help you understand the process of finding out what your congregation wants and deciding the best way to achieve that.

This book is also designed to help you choose a fund-raising partner. Once you begin uncovering what your congregation wants, you will find that it will be an expensive proposition. In my experience, churches that embark on a campaign on their own or use part-time counsel will typically raise one times annual giving. That begs the obvious question, "If you can do it on your own and raise the same amount as with part-time counsel, why would you ever pay for part-time counsel?" Perhaps having a little support is worth the money to some churches. The rest of this book is designed to outline what a respectful and reputable fund raiser will bring to your campaign.

Main Messages

Understand the church that you are.
Envision the church you want to be.
Detail what you need to become that church.

CHAPTER 2

Pre-campaign Planning: Charting Your Course

Establishing the Need:

There are two types of programs that can be conducted, either sequentially or in parallel, to help you decide if a campaign is needed. They are complimentary and therefore I recommend them sequentially, however some conduct them simultaneously. One is a needs assessment and the other is a discernment program. The needs assessment is designed to gather information from the members of various church groups. Discernment is a program for the church leadership to discuss the information gathered. You can just have a discernment program and gather input from the various ministry leaders, but I think it is important for the various organizations to ask their members rather than speak on their behalf without the elicited input.

I will address the needs assessment first. In general, there are two types of needs assessments: those that are done internally and those that involve outside counsel. Internal assessments are difficult to conduct and rarely result in useful information. They tend to be town hall-like meetings, which can degrade quickly into mayhem as hot-button issues in the church are raised. If a church member leads the session, it is difficult to control things without offending someone and creating hard feelings. Obviously, I do not encourage a self-assessment.

Churches that involve outside counsel typically engage either an architect or a fund-raising consulting firm to help them determine what they need to do. Certainly, I recommend using fund-raising consultants as I feel these consultants can help develop a global view of the project rather than focusing on buildings. Whoever is chosen must have extensive experience with church campaigns to fully grasp the complexities. The objective of the assessment process is to develop a comprehensive list of current church needs, not just building needs. This process should include interviewing all existing ministry committees separately to determine current facility, staffing, ministry, and financial needs from each perspective. By including all of the members of the various committees, you also begin to develop ownership in the issues that are being addressed. The key is to solicit information from each committee member.

In a recent United Methodist church campaign, a needs assessment was conducted with the choir. The music director voiced concerns over the youth music program and a need for a new piano. Others within the choir complained about the church acoustics. Others were concerned that the choir robes had been repaired so many times there were stitches on stitches. From that one meeting with one group, four needs were identified: an assistant choir director for youth programs, a new piano, a potential redesign of the sanctuary ceiling for acoustic improvement versus a new sound system, and new choir robes.

The liturgical committee needs assessment identified an area in the back of the church where the acoustics did not allow the congregation to hear the sermon. The committee members were also concerned that they were losing the teenager involvement in services.

This same type of meeting was conducted with every major group in the church. Each leader of each ministry then brought his list to the discernment meeting, and a comprehensive list of needs/wants was created. The leaders then identified overlapping concerns, including the church acoustics and concerns for youth programs.

As I wrote earlier, a discernment program is designed especially for the church leaders. It is a process at which the leaders of various ministries come together and discuss their needs and wants. This is where the list that was created in each needs assessment is brought forward.

A meeting such as this is best conducted away from the church, away from distractions. Many churches choose some type of retreat center. The meeting is best directed by an objective consultant who will motivate everyone to think outside the box and focus on vision. An outsider might also recognize common problems between ministry members that might otherwise be overlooked by those too close to the problems. At the same time, the consultant should keep the participants on track to accomplish their tasks of reviewing and prioritizing all of the needs and consolidating common problems that can be addressed by a single solution. In the scenario that was just described, the leaders decided that a new sound system would answer the needs of both the choir and the liturgical committee, and a youth music director would aid the struggling youth ministry and music.

Members of the building and finance committees should be present at the discernment meeting to answer any immediate logistical questions, for example, should the sanctuary be expanded or does the church need to purchase new property? It is especially important for members of the finance and building committees to hear firsthand from other leaders the intent of their needs/wants so that nothing is lost in translation. At the conclusion of this process, the church leadership should have a comprehensive list of the needs/wants of the various ministries along with a list of proposed solutions.

Through this seemingly simple process, you have now answered the question of what you need and you have begun the process of developing ownership among your congregation. I say it is seemingly simple because if you have everyone participating in one of these meetings, it can be overtaken by personalities or hot button issues unless an outsider can control the session. The goal of this meeting is to hear every ministry chair, unify the list of needs, and unify the purpose of the campaign to meet the needs. Avoiding confrontation is the job of the consultant. Let your consultant be the bad guy, cutting off discussion that gets into "the weeds" and away from the main thrust of the effort. Do not allow a member, or staff, of the church to become a target in these meetings.

I can't overemphasize the importance of conducting a thorough and comprehensive needs assessment that leads to a discernment process. The "buy-in" or "ownership" you gain from this process is invaluable in the course of a campaign. In my experience, congregations that skip this step shoot themselves in the foot. They don't lay the groundwork for the campaign and in the end don't garner the ownership they should have created. It is so powerful to go back to ministry leaders and say, "You mentioned that this was a critical need." They know they were heard, you heard them, and it was a need they addressed. Doesn't it make sense that you should try to get buy-in from everyone?

Moving Forward:

Now you know what the leadership wants/needs, you can extrapolate that the members of the respective committees want/need the same things because they went through the needs assessment process. It is now time to find out what it would cost if you did everything. If you have decided to renovate or build, now is the time to get an architect to tell you if the plan is possible. You will also need to collect a list of other estimated costs, such as a new sound system and the cost of its installation. At the conclusion of the process, you should have a comprehensive list that looks something like the following, depending on your needs (Table 1).

Table 1

Estimated Breakdown of Costs	
Deferred Maintenance Issues	$2,500,000
Tuck pointing stone	
Plastering & painting	
Stained-glass restoration	
Heating & cooling system	
Exterior & interior door refurbishment	
Roof repair	
Choir floor replacement	
Replace lintels & stone	
Exterior Vision	$2,250,000
Main entry & arrival area	
Children's play area	
Contemplation garden	
Replacement of the steeple	
Flagstone replacement at front entrance	
Landscaping & parking lot repairs	
Replacement of handicapped ramp	
Interior Vision	$5,500,000
Sanctuary sound, lights, & pew cushions	
Sanctuary wood refurbishing	
Renovation to vestry & parlor	
Great Hall sound system	
Handicapped accessibility	
Organ Replacement	$1,250,000
Mission & Outreach	$1,400,000
A 10 percent tithe to mission projects	
Contingency Fund/Various Expenses	$1,500,000
A construction & renovation contingency	
Retirement of 1999 construction debt	
$400,000 building & renovation fund	
Permits	
Campaign expenses	
Total Proposed Vision Costs	$14,400,000*

This may not be what you set as your ultimate goal. This is the list that you are going to take to the congregation to provide an estimate of the overall identified needs.

A good consultant will assist in leading you to an architect who can develop the conceptual plans. Included in the plans should be a proposed floor plan and a layout of the property site. Rough elevated renderings should be drawn. With all of this, an estimate of costs should be calculated. Remember, these are merely conceptual drawings, and cost should be kept to a minimum. Plans often change during this time and it would be foolish to spend a great deal of time, money, and energy on architectural drawings that will probably be altered in the coming months.

I was called to consult with an Episcopal church in Virginia where the leadership had hired an architect to design a much-needed addition. The architect designed an ultramodern addition to a very traditional, historic sanctuary. He went forward with his computer-aided designs to show the building from all angles. The cost for this service was $45,000. When I saw the design, I didn't think it fit with the design of the church and I knew we did not need all the computer-generated effects, but I was there to help test the need for the new addition to the church. At the end of the Focus Group Meetings, 100 percent of the congregation said they needed an addition and the same 100 percent said that the proposed addition was not what they wanted. The architect called me at home and asked me to encourage the church to move forward with the design, saying that when it was built, the congregation would love it. I laughed and told him that he must not have much experience with churches. I informed him that you can't make a congregation move forward, and without the support of the congregation there would be no funds to build. Ultimately, the church had to hire a new architect. Despite the unnecessary $45,000 expense and a four-month break waiting for the new designs, we ultimately enjoyed a very successful campaign.

Selecting an Architect:

Ensure that the architect you hire has done work with church groups in the past. While architectural firms that have not worked with churches may tell you that a church group is no different from any other group they have worked with, this is simply not true. A church, like a home, is very personal to most of the congregation. It is much more than just a building; it is a personal place of worship. To many, it is a place where they married, baptized their children, and buried their parents. An architect needs to understand that. Know that architects like to fully design a project. Ensure that you contract only for conceptual drawings of a site plan, floor plans, proposed elevated rendering, and an estimated breakdown of costs. Since these plans will be tested in Focus Group Meetings and changes are anticipated, they should not be so complete that the congregation feels they cannot suggest changes. Also, the more complete the plans are, the more invested the architect may be in the design and you may get resistance from him/her to change them. The architect must also be responsive. It should seem that your project is the most important one on which the architect is working, even if that is not the case. There is no set fee for an architect; you must factor that in the choice you make and may benefit by speaking to some other churches in your area that have recently built or renovated. As with any contract you sign, read it carefully. Your consultant must be able to work with the architect and, in many cases, will refer your church leaders to architects with church experience.

During an Episcopal church campaign in the Washington DC area, the rector encouraged me to visit with the architect to ensure the renderings and other materials were going to be ready for the Focus Group Meetings. In the hour I met with him, we discussed the current project as well as some leads I provided on church projects going on in the community. I felt it was a pledge of good faith to help him in his career. The architect was very grateful for the leads and I thought nothing of the time I had spent with him. A few days later, the rector informed me the architect charged the church $250 for the hour I spent with him. Needless to say, I was angry, especially given that during the conversation, our attention had turned to several potential church building projects for his firm. I have since warned churches to read the architectural contracts very carefully for hidden costs such as this.

Choosing a Stewardship Partner:

In a United Methodist church in Maryland, one of the members had prior "experience" in fund raising. She had spent the prior two years organizing the current building campaign. The woman had gathered a group of successful professionals whom she was certain could pull off a building campaign without outside help. They had met from time to time to discuss the plans, but nothing ever went beyond those meetings. I happened to call upon the church, and the pastor informed me that they were planning to build and had been working on it for a couple years. I made a presentation to him and a key lay leader. The two embraced our services and the organization of our campaign method. I then made a formal presentation to the church board, and the only one who voted against us was the woman who had been leading the effort for two years. She was determined not to pay the fee for a consultant when she was certain they could do the project on their own if given a little more time. The pastor was diplomatic and instrumental in explaining to the board that two years had come and gone with nothing to show for it. It was obvious that while well meaning, the committee lacked the organization skills to take on such a project. In the end, the chair leading the floundering effort was outvoted. When the church raised more than ten times annual giving, she told me how happy she was to be overruled. To this day, she sends me tickets to the church's annual spring event, and my whole family attends.

For obvious reasons, it is difficult for me to be very objective in this section. I believe that the method of campaign my firm employs not only raises more money, it also raises the spirit of the church. My plan encourages unity and team building. We encourage ownership, not delegation. I can only tell you of my success and where I have seen others fail. Even though I would consider a one to two times annual giving campaign a failure, many pastors do not because that is what the consultant they hired told them to expect. Many other fund raisers are masters at managing a church's expectations. They tell you what they can help you accomplish and, clearly, that is all they are going to help you accomplish.

Many times I have followed another firm's presentation of their plan and had the church committee say to me, "We were just informed that anyone who tells us that we can raise more than three times our annual giving is lying." The first few times it happened, I was surprised. I have since documented all of our success stories. Initially, the stories are met with skepticism. After a church calls our references, I tend to get a call that the members can't believe our results. My typical response is, "Let me help you believe." We now have a collection of so many success stories that five times annual giving is catching on as the benchmark to which all Capital Campaigns should be compared.

> I presented my Plan of Campaign to the leaders of a United Methodist church with an annual giving of about $250,000. I told these leaders that by using our method of stewardship, they could expect to raise five times their annual giving. The pastor told me that that would not be enough for the needs they had. The total cost of the new parish hall was over $4 million. I informed him that five times would be a wonderful achievement, and he convinced me that we would have to think bigger. Not used to being the one who is pushed, I was a little nervous as this pastor poured his heart and soul into this campaign and ignited the spirits within his congregation. In the end, they raised eighteen times their annual giving, $4.5 million, and I again learned not to tell people what they can't do.

However, if you have a member of the congregation who is experienced in fund raising and can devote adequate time to the campaign, you may not need outside counsel. This would be a terrific scenario for most churches because it would keep costs low. However, there are some true pitfalls to this approach. If your volunteer is not performing, are you going to fire him? After all, he is volunteering. If the campaign is not progressing or he has a family emergency, what happens? Are you willing to put the needs of the entire congregation in the hands of an amateur?

Can this member of the church truly be objective regarding the needs? If he/she tries to lead the congregation members in a direction that they are resisting, will there be hard feelings? If the member hears things that he/she thinks you won't like to hear, will you be told? How might you guarantee the confidentiality of the campaign records? Will this person be privy to all the pledged amounts?

In the end, churches that attempt a campaign on their own, no matter how good their "experienced" volunteer is, will usually raise one times annual giving, assuming the effort ever gets off the ground.

If you choose to hire outside counsel, a move I highly encourage, you need to select an experienced firm that is going to be your partner in this journey. The firm must have experience in Christian stewardship. The firm should work on an at-will contract, so that if for any reason the campaign is going slowly or something dramatic happens that puts the campaign on hiatus, you are not committed to paying for services when you cannot use them. The following is the story of a church that learned a very valuable but costly lesson, one that you will hopefully not have to learn yourself.

> An Episcopal church in Virginia used a part-time firm to help with a building campaign. The fund-raising firm did not believe in conducting a Feasibility Study; instead, it encouraged the church leaders to begin the Capital Campaign immediately. Unfortunately, the project was not well thought out and there was little ownership within the congregation. Three weeks into the effort, the decision was made to end the attempt. Unfortunately, the church had signed a contract with the part-time firm for the entire length of the campaign. Even though the effort ended abruptly and in disaster, the firm demanded payment. The church paid a fee of over $100,000.
>
> In contrast, with all of the hurricane activity in the 2005 season, our church clients in Florida opted to take time off from the campaign. With an at-will contract, there was no negative consequence. When they were ready to resume the campaign, our consultant returned promptly.

Since you are still reading, let's presume now that you have decided to use outside counsel. I will now outline the various types of service. They are full-time consulting and part-time consulting. How do you decide which is best for you and your congregation?

First, you have to establish what you need to raise to do the things you need or want to do. The next step is to look at your annual giving. Most part-time firms do not believe in conducting either a needs assessment or a discernment program because those types of meetings are time intensive and tie up one of their consultants.

If you only need up to one times annual giving, you could hire a part-time firm or do it yourself; the results are generally the same. If you need more than one times annual giving, then I highly recommend a full-time consulting firm. If you consider return on investment, part-time consulting could cost you up to 20 percent of what you raise. Most part-time firms generate one times annual giving, and charge an average of 10 percent of the church's annual budget. With a full-time consultant raising five times that of the part-time firm, your overall consulting costs decrease to approximately 2 to 4 percent.

Be very wary of any firm or individual that offers to be compensated based on a percentage of the funds pledged. This is highly unethical and encourages the consultant to put pressure on church members for higher amount gifts.

> In a home visitation to ask a church member for $100,000, she confessed that that would be a significant amount of her retirement and that she would be much more comfortable contributing $50,000. The pastor and I gladly accepted the generous pledge and left. In the car on the way back to the church, the pastor admitted that while he initially thought that it would be an advantage to work with a firm that worked on a percentage to motivate them to get more money for the project, that would not have been the best thing for this woman or the church. He was grateful for a firm that was working on a flat fee and in the best interest of the church.

How do you find a Capital Campaign consulting firm?

You can look on the Internet and pick a few to interview, or you can call around to area churches that have done campaigns and ask for recommendations. You can call your conference or diocesan development office and ask if there is a recommended firm. In the end, you are going to have to choose from a few recommended firms and interview them to see which method best suits your expectations.

During this interview process, you need to learn a few things about the firm, decide if the consultant is a good fit with your church, and decide if you like the approach. Remember that the consultant the firm brings does not have to be the one who does the campaign if you don't like him/her. The other point to consider is that "your" consultant may be placed into another campaign if you don't move quickly.

Some essential questions that I have provided to churches to assist them in making a decision include:

> 1. Does the firm provide full-time or part-time service? In follow-up, ask why the type of service it provides is superior to others. If the representatives don't think it is superior, why do they offer it?
> 2. What is the average length of a campaign for a church our size? How does that compare with churches of other sizes? What factors drive whether a campaign is shortened or lengthened?

3. Will your consultant be available to us to meet our volunteers' needs, or will we have to arrange our volunteers around the day the consultant is scheduled to be at our church?

4. Will your service provide us with a consultant who can accompany us on personal visits and presentations to prominent church members? If the schedule changes at the last minute, will the consultant be flexible?

5. Do you feel that there is value to your participation in a Readiness Assessment/Feasibility Study before the campaign, or could we do one on our own? If you can do one, does the church leadership need to be involved? Would you favor conducting more personal interviews or more group meetings? How do you structure such a meeting?

6. (If applicable) Before the Readiness Assessment/Feasibility Study, does your firm help us, or should we anticipate preparing on our own until you arrive for the first meeting?

7. What is the cost for this preliminary work provided by your firm?

8. What is the number one reason we should choose your firm? The amount of money you raise? The impact your service has on the volunteers? The length of the campaign?

If you have read the previous section of this book, you know some of these are trick questions. How a firm answers is very telling of the service it will provide during the campaign.

After hearing the difference in the types of service offered, you have to decide how much time and effort you can expect to be contributed by the members of your church to the administration of the campaign.

No matter what any consulting firm tells you, someone at the church is going to be responsible for the campaign 100 percent of the time. If you have a full-time consultant, your church members or pastor will not be the one drafting letters, training volunteers, picking up brochures, and contacting speakers; the consultant is doing that work. Some firms will encourage you to hire an additional staff person to assist in the campaign. This ultimately means you are paying the consulting firm to instruct you on how to add to your staff. Between the part-time firm's fee and the salary of a new and inexperienced employee to provide assistance in the fund raising and bookkeeping to achieve one times annual giving, this tends to be the costliest way to conduct a campaign.

Whomever you ultimately choose, ensure that he will help you do all of the following:

During the Readiness Assessment/Feasibility Study:

1. The consultant should help you collate the data and develop an effective Case for Support.

2. The consultant should not only coach all of your focus group presenters and write the scripts, but also should attend every Focus Group Meeting and take notes on the comments during the question and answer section.
3. The consultant should also accompany you, if desired, to any personal interviews.
4. The consultant should develop an effective questionnaire and tabulate the responses for his final report to you.
5. Finally, he should prepare a professional final report that you and the leaders can discuss regarding next steps.

It is important for the consultant to be involved in the Focus Group Meetings to answer questions that arise. While this is not the best time to give detailed information about a potential campaign, church members need to hear about the options of moving forward with a Capital Campaign based on a three-to five-year pledging period.

For the Campaign:

1. Develop a Plan of Campaign:
The consultant should present to you job descriptions for each of the key campaign members and help to identify and recruit the right leader for each position. Since your consultant has been involved in the Focus Group Meetings and has met many of the potential campaign leaders, the consultant should be invaluable in recommending individuals for the important leadership roles. Assistance should be provided in organizing the campaign committees, and he should attend any session when requested. The consultant should create a campaign calendar that should coordinate the activities of all committees.

2. Campaign Materials:
All printed materials, including the View Book, the Visitor's Handbook, and the campaign brochure, are key presentation tools and should be drafted by the consultant. Putting these materials together so that they are effective and concise and reflect the personality of the congregation is vital. This job should not be given to an amateur. The materials must be planned carefully so that they are ready at their needed time. As part of this, pledge cards must be designed and printed and you need someone who is there to oversee that they are right and on time.

3. Education & Coaching:
A full-time consultant gives you flexibility. His schedule belongs to you for the duration of the campaign. Training sessions can be conducted when it is convenient for your members, not just when the consultant happens to be available. He can respond to changes in scheduling and meetings for personal visits. He is also there to continually monitor the progress of the various committees and foresee and warn or respond at once to potential concerns or emergencies.

One of the consultant's primary responsibilities is to coordinate training of all individuals who will be visiting church members to secure their campaign pledge.

4. Campaign Reports/Records:
   You can keep your finger on the pulse of the campaign by reading the weekly report that your consultant should turn in to you and the other appropriate leaders. The consultant will keep the pledge card report and gift records up to date and oversee the timely sending of thank you letters to contributors. He will also submit a final report to you on the entire campaign effort.

5. Postcampaign Procedures:
   At the end of the time for which you have hired the consultant, he will turn over all materials to you and your staff and provide training to keep the campaign alive. For a few months after the campaign, the consultant will periodically call to check on the progress at no charge.

> I overheard a competing part-time fund raiser talking to a pastor about the service his firm could provide. The pastor asked, "How often is the consultant actually at the church during the campaign?" The fund raiser responded, "As often as you think you need us."

I think it is essential that a consultant is in residence for the duration of the project. You could certainly have a part-time consultant, whom you are paying $1,500 per day plus expenses, fly back and forth as needed. However, if you haven't been through a campaign before and aren't certain of the exact needs, how will you know to call him before the campaign is in real trouble? Aren't you hiring an experienced consultant so that he can tell you what is needed and anticipate problems? Many of the part-time firms will tell you that they can manage your campaign in six on-site visits. If you divide their fee by the number of times they are at your church, you can be paying $10,000 a visit or more.

I see these as the essential differences between full-time and part-time consulting.

Resident-Directed, Full-time Consulting	Part-time Consulting
Available any time 24/7 to the volunteers and church staff. Personal attention is given to the client in all phases of the campaign.	Time is divided among multiple clients. As many as 8 to 10 projects at once. No client enjoys exclusive personal attention.
Campaign is of shorter duration. Volunteers remain enthusiastic and committed.	Usually several months longer in duration. Lengthy campaigns can overburden and exhaust volunteers.
Campaign potential of 5 times annual giving. Results have often been substantially beyond that range.	Limited potential. Usually raising 1-2 times annual giving.
On-site and available to monitor and address all campaign issues as they arise.	Off-site and not available to identify potential concerns which arise. Unable to address unanticipated concerns immediately.
Personally observes campaign progress and determines where professional experience is needed.	Relies on volunteers to identify areas that need attention.
Available when volunteers require coaching. All meetings occur at convenience of volunteers.	Training and meeting times are subject to the availability of the part-time Director. Schedule must compete with other church campaigns.
Prepares all campaign materials for client approval.	Church staff and volunteers must complete all campaign work.
Director worships regularly with church members and participates in the life of the congregation.	Usually not available on Sunday. Director only available over telephone or through email between visits.
Fees and expenses are predictable and controlled.	In addition to campaign fees and expenses, church client is usually responsible for additional items such as airfare, hotel, auto rental, telephone calls, and meals.

I was the second of two firms to present to an Episcopal church committee in Indiana. After I finished my presentation, the pastor thanked me. I asked about the other firm that presented and the pastor rolled her eyes. She said that the consultant came into the meeting flustered and frustrated because his plane had been delayed. He then went on to complain that he was exhausted from running between the ten campaigns he was currently directing. The pastor informed me that our approach, one consultant focused on one campaign, was a welcome prospect. We did get the opportunity to direct that very successful campaign.

After you interview consulting firms, you will need to choose one based on the response to your plans and personalities. There may be strong opinions within the church leadership. You need to listen to all of them and then vote.

Many firms talk a good game of how you need to keep praying and God will provide. I firmly believe God helps those who help themselves, and the harder you work, the luckier you become. I have deep faith in Christ, but do not always wear it on my sleeve. My firm provides teaching in practical stewardship growth skills to the volunteers involved in the campaign. Their mission is to then use those skills to teach others. As Christians, we have a deep sense of obligation to our church and our communities, and learning skills in stewardship development is as important as praying for money to be contributed to the church.

At a Church of Christ sales presentation, I asked the pastor to lead us in prayer to start the meeting. The meeting progressed per my usual agenda and at the end, the pastor stated that we were the last of the five firms interviewed. She went on to say that the other firms came to the meetings with a very spiritual message of trusting in the Lord and in our faith. They went on evangelizing about the power of prayer and how that was the most crucial aspect of a "true Stewardship Campaign." The pastor stated that my message showed a practical approach to stewardship. My heart sank as I had heard others state that I wasn't as spiritual in my presentation as other firms. She then looked at me and said, "You are the only one that asked us to start the meeting with a prayer, and that is faith in action." To my joy, we were selected to conduct the project.

The last point I am going to make in this section involves the campaign committee. It is too early to preselect them at this phase. You will certainly have people jockeying for the positions and others trying to run from the positions. Resist the temptation to promise the positions to anyone. Allow your experienced consultant to help you identify leaders through the Feasibility Study process. You will most definitely find many diamonds in the rough.

Main Message

Even if you have been involved in a campaign in the past, you will need a
qualified, dedicated partner through this process.
Choose your partner carefully and fully understand the service you will be
getting. Discounted prices tend to reflect discounted service. Seldom is the
cheapest product the best.
Let a professional help your congregation leaders compile a list of their needs
and wants, then let him help the leadership package their vision and test it in
a Feasibility Study.

CHAPTER 3

Making It Happen:

The Four Main Ingredients

T he term stewardship comes from the word steward, which means custodian or keeper. What are we in custody of? What are we keeping? Most would say our faith. Therefore, a stewardship campaign is a way of keeping or growing the faith. Over time, the term has been often equated more with the financial aspect of the project, as needed or wanted ministries have come to require more funding. Funds are the focus of most stewardship campaigns, but should not be the sole focus. A stewardship campaign is an opportunity to grow the facilities, to enhance the ministries, to elicit the input of church members, to identify new lay leaders, to enhance relationships among church members, and perhaps to decrease debt.

Stewardship and tithing are the not the same thing. The word tithe comes from the root tenth, meaning the first tenth of what you make belongs to God. Tithing is a term still used by some Christian churches, but it should be a base of giving. During a stewardship campaign, prayerfully considered gifts for specific purposes should be made in addition to the tithe amount.

Just to be clear: money isn't everything, and the mantra of time, talent, or treasure does hold true when it comes to stewardship. Not everyone should be held to the same amount of giving, but they should be held to the same consideration for their gift based on their ability. Ministries are funded by the generosity of the members of the congregation. It is an essential part of any campaign to find out what your congregation wants to support. It is also important to educate the congregation about what you already support. We cannot be passive about needed funding for important ministries. We must be bold and proud to serve and support the work of the church.

The highest levels of church leadership must have the firm conviction that the decision to conduct this campaign has evolved out of the vision, work, prayers, and planning of the church members and is dedicated to the glory of God. The basic aim of the campaign is to go beyond fund raising. The leaders seek to broaden the base of Christian stewardship, deepen the joy of commitment, motivate the member's spiritual lives, foster Christian fellowship, develop new leaders, and engage in special fellowship of daily prayer on behalf of these objectives.

There are four main ingredients of a successful Capital Campaign. There is overlap between the ingredients, and eventually they all blend. All are essential to success and no one item is more important than the others.

The first is the **Case Statement.** It is the clear, concise reason that you members should support the campaign. The Case Statement is developed after you have been through all of the meetings with all of the individual groups and met with your church leadership to discuss all of the reasons for a campaign. This is the place where the church leaders must lead. Difficult decisions must be made; you need to be ready to explain why some courses of action were chosen over others. Whether you have decided to acquire property, to renovate, to build, to pay off debt, or to increase your missions and outreach, this is the place where you reword your decisions and make the case understandable for the congregation. In addition to the proposed floor plans, property site plan, and a good estimate of costs, it is important to include how current ministries will be enhanced or how new ministries will be provided. Far too often, the focus is on the bricks and mortar aspect of the project; ministries should be the motivating concern.

The second ingredient is **leadership**. Although as a group you have chosen a course of action, you have to ensure that all the leaders understand and agree to the most crucial and urgent needs and believe in the proposed solutions. It is important that members of the church council or vestry are involved. In addition, the building and finance committees must support and be involved with the project. You will probably have church council members who tell you that they think the building project and Capital Campaign are mistakes. These are often people who don't want to make a contribution or do not want to incur any additional work load. You need to convince them that there is enough evidence that changes are wanted by the church committees and are a reflection of the wants of the congregation. Assure them that you will test the plan with the congregation before moving forward. If the congregation is in support, how can these people be right? Convince them to at least allow the congregation to hear the plan. If they absolutely refuse, allow them the opportunity to graciously step down from the church council. There are people who will never be won over and will serve as a constant thorn throughout the campaign.

You will be tempted in these early meetings to try to identify the leader of the campaign, the Campaign Chair. Resist that temptation. Your Campaign Consultant should be able to help you identify the Campaign Chair. This is important because it is the Campaign Consultant who will ultimately pledge his/her support to the chair to let him know that the consultant will do the bulk of the work.

The next ingredient is your **constituency**. You need to engage all members of the church, not just the regular attendees, and certainly not just the ones who pledge to the Annual Campaign. Even if you have members who participate only a few times a year, include them; you never know who has a history with a church that predates you. You will need to send a letter to all those people announcing the Focus Group Meetings. Your consultant should develop the letter. The key to this letter is to send out a teaser message. The common mistake is to send out a letter outlining the entire plan. If you send out a lengthy letter with the plan, members feel that they have already been informed and therefore do not need to attend the meetings. The teaser message should be something like: "Our building committee has been working on immediate and long-range plans, and is now ready to present those plans for discussion. The opinions of the congregation are important." Some pastors are very bold and include a line that says, "I expect you to be there." Some pastors want to include only those members who are most active and attend church regularly. Others are willing to include everyone who has ever attended. Although many pastors in areas where there are seasonal members tend to want to hold off on conducting the campaign until most members are in town, the snowbirds are typically not the largest donors to the campaign. Most of the time, it only slows down your timing to wait until the seasonal members arrive. However, as the following story illustrates, there is merit in personally visiting and challenging seasonal members.

In a recent Lutheran church campaign, one of the most prominent families lived in the community only a few months each year. The rest of the time, they were farther north where they had lived most of their lives and where their grandchildren now lived. The pastor waited to meet with them personally to explain the building project in detail. Most leaders of the campaign were skeptical of any meaningful gift since the family was not really involved in the church. Even though they were only part-time members of the congregation, they were happy to meet with the pastor and ultimately made the lead gift to the campaign. They offered an additional and equally generous contribution to be used as a challenge to the year-round members. Their involvement and inspirational giving was instrumental in the success of this project.

The final ingredient is the **Plan of Campaign**. This is a process implemented by an experienced consultant. It must be a well-tested and proven plan that starts with taking the case to the congregation members for input and then over time, engaging them step by step, asking them to prayerfully consider an inspirational and sacrificial gift to the needs of the church.

Another important element in the Plan of Campaign is the timing of all aspects of the effort. I am asked frequently, "When should we conduct our campaign?" My response usually is, "Right after we finish a thorough Feasibility Study." While most church leaders think there is something magical about a fall campaign, the fact is that the best time to conduct your Capital Campaign is when you and the other church leaders are prepared to make this endeavor their top priority for several months.

In some cases, depending on the area of the country you live, it may be a good idea to wait until better weather. Minnesota in the winter and Florida in the summer may be difficult times for campaigns. However, having said that, I have personally directed projects in those places at those times with great results.

The point that I am making is that every church and location is different. It is not as important to look at the calendar to make a decision on when to begin as it is to determine the availability of the leaders and congregation as a whole. The next section will discuss how we test whether those four ingredients are in place and if you should move forward with a campaign or go back to the drawing board.

Main Message

There are four ingredients to make a successful campaign: Case Statement, Leadership, Constituency, and a Plan of Campaign. All elements must be present and in place to proceed.

CHAPTER 4

Readiness Assessment/Feasibility Study:
Taking the Case to the People

In a recent discussion with the development director of a United Methodist conference, I was told that the conference was planning to raise $20 million for the sole purpose of starting new churches throughout the conference. I explained to the director that that need should be tested through a thorough Feasibility Study that would uncover needs that local churches would perceive as urgent. Then I was told that the decision of the needs for the campaign had already been made and that the campaign would only be for new church starts. "People will give because it is the right thing to do," the director emphatically added. I wished him the best of luck, knowing in my heart that this was going to be a disaster for him and the conference. A few months later, the campaign was abandoned. There is no place for arrogance in church fund raising. I was commended by a Methodist church leader for not taking advantage of what could have been a lucrative situation for my firm.

A Readiness Assessment, otherwise known as a Feasibility Study, is an essential part of the process. Its main objective is to test the plan that the leaders have decided will best address the current and urgent needs of the church. It is not a town hall meeting asking for all new ideas, although any suggestions are collected and considered. The objective is to test the feasibility of the church leaders' proposed plan. Why is it needed? It only makes sense to test the case before you proceed to a campaign.

First, the assessment is used to evaluate if the congregation agrees with the leadership's view of the status of facilities, programs, etc. of the church. It can happen that the leadership is too close to the problems and is focusing on one need when the rest of the church sees the true problem as something else entirely. Second, the process allows the church members to identify strengths and weakness in the case. Through this process, the congregation members can help prioritize what they identify as the most important needs. Third, differing viewpoints can be heard about current church needs and programs. This opportunity to allow members to voice concern and to provide the leaders a chance to respond can be very beneficial. In some cases, individuals just want their concerns heard and acknowledged. It is important to let everyone have their say during this process. Often, differences are a merely a matter of miscommunication and can be addressed and rectified prior to the start of a campaign.

Some secondary objectives that are achieved in this process involve developing ownership in the ideas among the congregation, discovering new leaders, and creating an excitement that the leadership is leading.

> During a Feasibility Study for a church campaign in California, the leadership was testing support from the congregation for both a new heating and cooling system and the purchase of some property across the street for a new parking lot. Neither of these items was especially exciting to the congregation. However, during one of the Focus Group Meetings, the music director stated that if she had her way, there would be a new organ in the sanctuary. This electrified the congregation. The organ was added to the case along with the heating and cooling system and parking lot. With the organ project leading the way, enough funds were secured to pay for the organ, the heating and cooling system, the parking lot, and the creation of an endowment. Truth be told, I am certain that nearly everyone signing a pledge card was thinking about the new organ when they made their decision on what to contribute.

Some fund-raising consulting firms will offer to do personal interviews with your most affluent members on their own. They say they don't want you to "waste your time" conducting this preliminary business. They also say that prospective donors will not offer an open and honest assessment of the project if a staff member or volunteer is present. Don't fall into this trap. The fact is, a Readiness Assessment, or Feasibility Study should be used to assist in convincing prospective donors that there is a significant need that must be addressed. It is an opportunity to pre-sell a campaign effort and to enlist support. A hired consultant who has no relationship with the individual being interviewed cannot be expected to help lay the groundwork necessary for a successful campaign effort. It can send the wrong message to members of the church to have a hired consultant take the place of a fellow church member. Therefore, I would recommend that church leaders resist the temptation to send consultants to conduct interviews. Even though it seems

appealing, how do you know what they are asking or how many people they are really seeing? How do you know that what they are relaying to you is accurate or in the spirit in which it was said? Of course it is in their best interest to put a positive spin on the comments; they want you to proceed with a campaign and continue to pay them. These are the reasons that lay leaders or clergy should accompany consultants on all interviews. It is a team effort and should be regarded as such.

My firm was recently called by a Methodist conference to conduct a Feasibility Study and Capital Campaign. Just a few months prior, the conference had contracted with a part-time fund-raising firm for a Feasibility Study. The members of the board liked the idea of allowing this firm to conduct all the personal interviews alone. They believed that the firm would target a large portion of the influential and affluent members of the conference. Several months passed, and a fee of $25,000 was paid to this firm. At the time of the Study Report, the board members were given the findings of the seventeen personal interviews. The board members were shocked at how few interviews were conducted and that people of influence and affluence were not represented among those chosen to be interviewed. The interviewed members were not known to have either influence or affluence. The findings were sketchy at best. However, the poor results did not deter this firm from recommending proceeding with a major conferencewide Capital Campaign. The question many board members had was, "How can you recommend such an aggressive campaign when you did not even meet with the conference's most wealthy and influential leaders?"

"We were not able to get in to meet with those individuals," the consultant said. "They were unwilling to schedule time with us."

The point is that individuals really don't want to meet with people they don't know. These fund raisers were hired guns, doing work the conference leaders should have been doing. At the time of our initial meeting, I informed the board that while we did not like to try to fix a problem like this, the good news was that little damage had been done since so few meetings had occurred. We assisted the conference with a genuine Feasibility Study with remarkable results. Only after this flawed attempt did the leaders of this conference understand how vital their role was in preselling and helping to create ownership in the proposed building project.

The leaders of the church must be present at these personal interviews and Focus Group Meetings. The consultant plays a major role and should help, but the leaders need to hear what their congregation, or constituency is saying. In addition, the consultant cannot deliver the message of the church leadership regarding the plan the way that a devoted member of the church can. If you are not involved, it sends a clear message that the leaders are not devoting time to this process. Is this the message you want to send?

> My firm was in the running for two campaigns in the same metropolitan area. One was on the outskirts of the city and the other was downtown. Both had annual giving of approximately $1 million and both had needs of about $6 million. At both interviews, I shared my method of Focus Group Meetings and personal interviews and told the leaders that if they did the campaign properly they could raise five times annual giving, approximately $5 million. The pastor of the downtown church was intrigued, but was intimidated by the work involved in my plan. The pastor of the suburban church embraced my plan and hired us. At the downtown church, a part-time firm was hired that had said there would be no need for the pastor's involvement until the start of the campaign. The part-time representative also told the church that he would be able to predict by the end of the study what the church could raise. The part-time firm drafted a letter to the congregation outlining the plan and soliciting feedback. In the letter, the consultant asked how much money members would contribute to this campaign. Approximately 30 percent of the letters were returned, according to the firm, and the consultant announced to the pastor that only $1 million could be raised. The campaign never took place because the pastor thought he did not have the congregation's support. The suburban church that hired my firm raised $6.5 million.

The failure and success of the two campaigns above rested in the execution of the Feasibility Study. In one, a letter was sent. There is nothing personal about a letter. The letter was not well received, as most letters soliciting funds are not. A letter also does not create a sense of either ownership or excitement among the congregation. In addition, the part-time consultant made the fatal mistake in a Feasibility Study; he asked what the respondents would give. This always baffles me. How can you ask what someone will give when you cannot even say what the final project is going to be? If asked upfront, without a solid, tested plan, most people will give a token amount, and once they write an amount down, they are unlikely to change it. This is why these firms can predict to within a few dollars what will be contributed to a campaign. This is also why their results are so poor.

> A Methodist church that asked me to come and present my Plan of Campaign shared with me the results of its last campaign. The church had used a part-time firm and had raised one times annual giving. I proceeded to speak about our Plan of Campaign and specifically how our Feasibility Studies are conducted. Immediately following my presentation, one of the leaders admitted that the church had made two fatal mistakes in its last campaign, based on my presentation. The first was that the Focus Group Meetings were not open to the entire church, only select families, creating a sense of exclusion. The second mistake was that the consultant insisted asking everyone following these preliminary meetings what they would pledge to the campaign. This generated token amounts and predicted the failure of the campaign.

As I have stated, there are two ways to approach the congregation. One is through Focus Group Meetings and the other is through personal interviews. Focus Group

Meetings are the preferred method and should be used to engage the majority of the congregation. Personal interviews can be reserved for church members who are unwilling to attend a group session or whose schedules won't accommodate one. Personal interviews can also be reserved for members who are particularly against any change in the church. Most church leaders know who they are. Rather than invite them to a meeting where they have a forum to sour the congregation against even hearing about change, it may be better to meet with them privately. This should not be used for more than a few select members of the congregation. I do not discourage dissent; I merely discourage the presence of those who will monopolize the meeting for their own agenda and waste the time of the other members of the congregation. I want to reiterate that it is critical for the church leadership to attend these meetings and hear what the congregation has to say about the plan. It's likely you will learn something about your church.

In a campaign in the South, I was scheduled to meet a prominent business leader in his office who could not afford the time to come to one of the Focus Group Meetings. I was to meet up with the Campaign Chairman to call on this affluent and influential member to present the case and get his reaction. After I waited twenty minutes and the meeting drew near, the Campaign Chairman had not arrived. I asked the secretary if I could reschedule the meeting, and she informed me that the businessman was going out of town for a few weeks. Knowing I would not be able to reschedule, and in a time before cell phones allowed me to check on the whereabouts of the Campaign Chair, I broke my own rule and met with this individual on my own. He told me nothing of his true thoughts on the case. When I met with the Campaign Chair later that day, he admitted to forgetting about the meeting. When I told him that I learned nothing from this individual and felt he might not even support the campaign, he was surprised. He knew this man had strong opinions about the church. I told the chairman that he probably could have elicited that information, but I certainly could not. It was a terrible missed opportunity for the campaign.

Length of the study:

The length of the study will vary by the number of members in your church. The more members, the more meetings you will need to have. You want to ensure that all members are invited and have been given the opportunity to attend, even if they do not take advantage of it. Ideally, you should have twenty-five to forty members per meeting. The time frames and typical number of meetings vary from four weeks and approximately twelve meetings for a church of seven hundred members to eight weeks and approximately twenty-two meetings for a church of three thousand members.

Who should present at the meeting?

A variety of people can present and, in fact, it is an excellent opportunity to identify and give some potential new leaders a chance to perform. Certainly, the senior pastor should be present to open with prayer. However, an articulate member of the congregation, trained by a seasoned consultant, should actually make the presentation. If you have a rising star in the congregation, someone very well liked, include him/her. If there is someone who has shown great interest in the project, that person is another good resource. People from the building or finance committees are typically safe choices because they are intimately familiar with why the case decisions were made. Including the architect can be very helpful when it is time to present the renderings. The key to the meeting is that the presenters are well prepared and practiced.

> In one campaign, a lawyer who had been instrumental in recruiting our firm to consult on the campaign and essential in recruiting the presenters for the Focus Group Meetings decided that it was not necessary for him to practice before presenting to the group. He was a lawyer, after all, who presented to groups for a living. Despite our encouragement, he would not practice. When the time came, he stood before the group and fumbled his way through a disjointed presentation and then stammered through his answers to the most common questions we had anticipated. At the conclusion of the presentation, he came over, sat down next to me and said, "You were right. I should have practiced."

Approximately a week or two prior to the dry run of the presentation, scripts should be distributed to six or eight potential presenters. Two of them should be identified as the ones who will present at the practice presentation, but everyone should practice on their own so they can help critique the two who will present. A few key leaders should be invited to the dry run to help formulate answers to questions that might stump the presenters.

Two presentations are needed. The first should be a brief history of the church. This perspective is designed for the newest members of the congregation, although the older members often enjoy hearing the story. It should include the age of the church and why it was founded, and it should end with a description of the current needs. The second presentation should explain how those needs are going to be addressed. These are the proposed solutions brought forth through the church leadership. Included in this talk is a detailed presentation of the floor plans and rendering, if a building project is included in the case.

The agenda of the meeting should roughly follow the outline below.

Welcome
Opening Prayer
History of the Church
Long-range Planning Process
Conceptual Master Plan

Question & Answer/Comment Session
Questionnaire Completion
Adjourn

In a recent Methodist campaign, one of the presenters decided that he should not proceed according to the agenda. He wanted to just open up the meeting to suggestions from the congregation. He told me that he liked my ideas, but thought that more direct input was needed. Having done this for many years and seen it done in so many ways, I offered him my perspective. I suggested that there were three main reasons for following the agenda:

1. If you just open the meeting up for discussion, it will appear that the leadership has not yet put any real thought into the needs of the congregation.
2. Doing so would defeat the purpose of the Feasibility Study, which is to test the plan that the leadership is proposing.
3. If people begin making new suggestions that in the end you do not incorporate, it will appear that you did not listen or value their ideas.

I again reminded him that this was not a town hall meeting. Our purpose was to test the plans that the church leadership had decided upon. I reassured him that if the people did not agree with the proposed plans, they would make it known. He conducted the Feasibility Study according to the agenda with great success.

Toward the end of the meeting, there is time allotted for completion of a short, pertinent questionnaire. Members should complete the questionnaire before they leave the meeting. Below are some sample questions:

1. In your opinion, what is the **most important** benefit to be realized as a result of the proposed building program for our church?
2. How would this building program help fulfill our mission?
3. Have we forgotten anything? Would you add anything to proposed plans?
4. A Capital Campaign requires many volunteers with varying responsibilities for its successful completion. Would you consider supporting a Capital Campaign?

   Financially? _____YES _____ NO _____ Need more information
   Volunteer Time? _____YES _____ NO _____ Need more information

5. Who would you suggest for leadership roles to ensure the success of a Capital Campaign?
6. My hope for my church is:
7. Do you have any additional comments regarding the proposed building program?

Notice that Question 3 fulfills the town hall meeting issue and allows someone to interject a new idea that was not presented. It also allows those who do not like to speak up in groups to have input. Most importantly, please notice that nowhere in any of this process are people asked how much they will pledge. This is important because these are still preliminary plans that are subject to change based on the outcomes of all of the meetings. When you ask for pledges, you should be asking everyone based on the same plans. If you ask at this time, the gifts will be spontaneous and will likely be token amounts, not inspirational. You should never request inspirational giving, nor should you expect anything but a token contribution if you do, until the right person is asking in the right way with the right materials.

> One of the lay leaders of a campaign was vacationing at the beach and bumped into one of the more affluent members of the congregation. The affluent member had participated in the Feasibility Study process and was very supportive of the campaign ideas. He had calculated that to meet the projected church needs, every family would have to pledge $25,000. The affluent church member confided to the lay leader that he felt particularly blessed and was going to pledge $35,000. The lay leader reported this information to the pastor and me when he returned from his vacation. With the case firmly established after the final Feasibility Study Meeting was complete, the pastor and I made the visit on this potential $1 million donor. With our View Book in hand and the pastor's practiced case presentation, the affluent member indeed pledged the one million dollars. He confided to us after the fact that he had only anticipated pledging $35,000. He said that had he been asked for his pledge during the Feasibility Study, he would have only pledged $35,000. He said that having seen the process of the Feasibility Study and now having the final case presented in a comprehensive and concise manner, he was happy to make one of the lead gifts. We were happy to have his pledge and a terrific start to the campaign.

Where and when are the Focus Group Meetings?

The Focus Group Meeting does not just happen on its own. There is preparation and church member involvement, which I will outline below. The venue is the first challenge.

> In a Lutheran campaign, one of the church leaders wanted to host a Focus Group Meeting at her home. Even though we wanted the meetings to be held at the church to ensure that everyone felt an equal opportunity to attend, she insisted. She created a large invitation list and hired caterers. Since she was planning the event without any input from the consultant, she neglected to secure parking in her downtown community. On the day of the meeting, after only four cars could park in her two-car driveway (no other parking was available), the other invited members abandoned the event.

I have found that these meetings draw the greatest attendance if they are held at the church following worship services. People are already there and there are no concerns about making additional trips or finding more parking or getting lost. You should schedule as many meetings as you are able to within the weeks of the study. Try to secure the same space for the entire duration of the study so there is no confusion as to where it is going to be held for the sake of your presenters, consultants, and congregation. Although the majority of meetings should be in conjunction with the end of a service, you might try having a few in the middle of the week during the evening for members with small children who can't stay around after the service or who have other obligations following the worship service.

You need to identify some church members who will serve as the hosts for the event. They greet attendees, facilitate signing in, and suggest that members sit toward the front of the room so they have a better view of the renderings. The hosts are also another layer of involvement that increases the feeling of ownership. The hosts will be able to answer some general questions about what is going to happen at the meeting. They should comment on the length of approximately one hour, who the presenters will be, whether the pastor will be attending, and that there will be a question and answer period and a short survey at the end. They can also comment that there will be no solicitation of funds at the meeting, that it is informational and educational, and that the congregation's views are critical.

The host's job is to promptly call the meeting to order and thank everyone for attending. He may deliver the opening prayer if the pastor is unavailable. The host will then introduce the first presenter. Toward the end of the meeting, the host should assist in distributing the questionnaire and pens, and then help collect them. He should thank everyone for attending and for their participation.

You must have the proposed floor plans and renderings ready in time for the presenters or the architect to practice and become familiar with the design and comfortable with walking people through it. The rendering should be dry mounted and placed on easels. In this day and age of technology, you are probably wondering why we don't just use computer-aided design and put the plan up on a screen. There are two reasons. First, it is easier to approach the renderings after the meeting for an up-close view if they are printed and displayed and second, the meeting can proceed even if there is a computer glitch.

So, it seems that the church members are doing the majority of the work thus far. I am sure you are wondering what the consultant is doing during the meeting. First, he got you organized and this far along; second, throughout the meeting he is taking copious notes about what people are saying. He will collect all of the questionnaires and tabulate the results. He will deliver to you at the end of the process a completely unbiased synopsis of what happened throughout the meetings. Included in the verbal and written report will be an assessment of the support he feels you have or do not have for the case. He will also deliver to you a list of names of possible Campaign Chairs and suggestions on other key leadership positions based on what he has seen and for whom the congregation showed support through the questionnaires. He will provide copies for you to deliver to the leadership so that you can discuss whether to revise and retest the plans, revise and move forward, or just move forward.

Main Message

After the leadership consolidates the list of wants and needs and collates costs with possible courses of action, allow the congregation members to decide what they will support.

CHAPTER 5

Administrative Issues of the Campaign:

An Overview

You have just completed your Feasibility Study and you have received the summary evaluation from your Campaign Consultant. You meet with him to determine whether there should be changes in the plan before you move forward. Because the focus of the Feasibility Study is to pre-sell the campaign to the congregation, we have never encountered a situation in which the church has not moved forward. I know of churches that have used other approaches to a feasibility study and reported that at the end of their study they had to abandon the plans because it was determined what could be raised was not nearly enough. I may sound like a broken record, but that is yet another reason why we don't ask what someone will give before we know the final plan.

You will receive the list of roles and responsibilities for the campaign leaders. Although the consultant should have names of potential leaders in mind, putting it in print can be tricky; if the list gets out before it is final, there could be problems. It's better to have those discussions with the pastor and the chair of the campaign, who must be the first recruited. Then enlist the other individuals. Identifying and recruiting the right and best possible individuals are keys to a successful campaign. It is never recommended to simply ask for volunteers to fill important leadership roles. More often than not, the best people for the task of leadership are those who may not necessarily desire the job. As the saying goes, you can lead a horse to water, but you can't make him drink. Of the many jobs of the Campaign Consultant, making the horse thirsty must be a primary goal.

Assuming you have decided to move forward, with or without revision of the case, you now need to more fully understand all of the leadership and administrative positions of the campaign and their respective responsibilities.

This chapter is designed to give you an overview of those responsibilities and provide information about choosing the best leader for each job, the materials that will be needed, the Scale of Gifts to achieve your identified needs, the campaign calendar, and the responsibility of training and coaching the volunteers on a daily basis.

Now that a Campaign Chairperson has been identified and recruited, it is time to enlist members of the Campaign Steering Committee. They have been identified through the Feasibility Study questionnaires and your consultant has given you a list based on what he/she saw during the Feasibility Study. If you select the others first, the chair may feel more like a figurehead than an integral part of the leadership of the campaign. Positive personal relationships between the campaign leadership are important. If they feel a personal commitment to the leadership, they won't let them down.

There are numerous jobs in the campaign. As we saw in the Feasibility Study, you can engage many members and distribute the work load while creating ownership. This is an opportunity to invite those members who might want to be involved but have not yet found their unique niche in the congregation. From choosing the leaders to helping them as they organize each committee, the consultant should be at your side. You would like to find one person for each key position, but there is nothing written in stone that only one person can be named as the chairperson of a particular phase of the campaign. Co-Chairs can be a great way to engage more leaders in the campaign, as well as to divide responsibilities and work load. In addition, Co-Chairs are a great idea in case of unexpected illness or necessary business travel of individuals.

> The person we felt would be an effective Pattern Gifts Chairman was identified and recruited. However, due to serious travel demands, he informed us that he did not have enough time to make the campaign a priority for the full period of time required. So, we helped him find a Co-Chair. After a little more time, it was clear that they needed a little more help, so the pastor convinced them to recruit their wives to help. In the end, the four of them did a great job.

The steering committee consists of people of influence and affluence whose involvement in the Capital Campaign inspire confidence that the effort will succeed. Past and present leaders of the church as well as a diverse representation from throughout the membership should be on this committee to guide the course of action during the campaign.

Responsibilities:

1. Work closely with the pastor, Campaign Chairperson(s), and the Campaign Consultant in developing and implementing the basic steps in the campaign plan.

2. Help identify and recruit key church members to serve in leadership positions.
3. Establish a pattern of prompt, thoughtful, and inspirational giving, encouraging others to do likewise.
4. Assure that committee members have made their pledges.
5. Give the Capital Campaign top priority during the coming weeks and months, performing duties promptly with diligence and enthusiasm. Attendance at all meetings demonstrates hearty backing and support and provides the active guidance necessary for success.
6. Assist in planning Capital Campaign Kick-off Event.
7. Assure that the entire congregation is kept informed of the campaign's progress.
8. Help identify and recruit those members who will visit other members to participate financially in the campaign.

Specific role responsibilities include:

The pastor's role is one of initiation, inspiration, and support of the Capital Campaign and the steering committee. He should commit to an inspirational gift to the campaign and then announce his financial support. Since the salary of the pastor is known, his gift will serve as a benchmark for others. Whether his salary is $40,000 or $140,000, it is a published number in the church budget. When the campaign begins, it is critical for the pastor to be seen as a leader, committed to the effort. The gift by the pastor can be inspirational to others.

> In a recent campaign in a small church where the pastor made $40,000 a year, he asked me what other pastors give to campaigns. I told him it varied based on ability. He asked me what I thought he would need to contribute over the five years to set an example of sacrificial giving. I told him that a $25,000 gift from him during that time would be inspirational. He took a deep breath and told me he would discuss it with his wife. The next day, when he and his wife were asked for their pledge, he informed us that he was deeply committed to the campaign. They pledged $30,000. The congregation was inspired and they raised eight times annual giving, far surpassing their goal.

The pastor must also show the importance of the campaign by attending all of the steering committee meetings. He will be critical in helping to recruit others to lead the campaign. Through sermons and personal interactions, he will create a sense of understanding and support for the campaign. He will participate in solicitation visits as needed and work closely with the Campaign Consultant to assist in decision making or to be apprised of various campaign issues. Typically, he will meet daily with the consultant.

In an Episcopal church, the pastor and I, in addition to our regular daily morning meeting, got together just before the Thursday night campaign meetings to discuss any last-minute concerns. After the group dispersed, the pastor and I met up at a coffee shop to talk about the meeting and strategize for the upcoming week. These meetings were a great opportunity to keep the pastor on track in all aspects of the campaign. The campaign was a great success and the church raised seven times annual giving. I am happy to report that fourteen years later, the pastor and I are still in contact and often recall the achievement of his campaign.

The Campaign Chairperson is the lay leader for the effort. He or she must be an individual who the clergy and congregation see as a natural leader within the church. It is best if the person has shown an interest in the campaign; however, the person of choice may have to be coaxed into assuming this leadership position. If the chair-select informs you that he has neither the time nor inclination to work on the project, try to find another leader. This job requires a commitment. Like the pastor, the chair should be prepared to give an inspirational gift to the campaign. He should preside over all steering committee meetings. He should help identify, recruit, and motivate other outstanding leaders to participate. The consultant will work as his right arm, making sure that the chair has all of the support he/she needs.

In a large Methodist church campaign, the pastor decided who he wanted to be the Campaign Chair even before the Feasibility Study was completed. His nominee was a well-known and well-respected business leader in the community. In private discussions, the pastor discovered that the man would accept the position reluctantly, but for personal reasons would not be a source for a large gift and would not be able to participate in all the committee meetings. The pastor was happy to merely have the man's name associated with the campaign. Toward the conclusion of the Focus Group Meetings, the pastor informed me of his choice. I had seen the man's name mentioned only twice on all of the questionnaires. I was immediately concerned, knowing that this was a recipe for disaster. I quickly offered the pastor an alternate, a committed, well-respected member whose name had been raised in numerous Focus Group Meetings as a respected, lay leader. This person had also expressed a keen interest in leading the campaign. The pastor refused. My arguments about leadership through presence in the campaign meetings as well as an inspirational gift as a sign of commitment as a signal to the other committee members almost seemed to fall on deaf ears. Finally, at my urging, he agreed to allow the other member to serve as Co-Chair. As the campaign progressed, the reluctant chair performed exactly as I had anticipated and was not a force for the campaign. The Co-Chair carried the campaign and ultimately the effort was a great success, something in which the reluctant chair took great pride.

The **Advance Gifts Chairperson** is responsible for securing major gifts that will represent 50 to 60 percent of the campaign goal. The chair of this committee, like all campaign leaders, should be willing to make an inspirational gift. The chair should recruit persons of influence and affluence who will feel comfortable asking peers to make inspirational gifts that will assure the success of the campaign. He will divide the selected members into teams, each with a captain and team members to call on the identified church members. The team captain will solicit pledges from the team members. He should assure adequate orientation, training, and coaching of team members prior to their selection of prospects. He also should oversee their selection of prospects to determine whether another team member may be better suited to call on a prospect. This phase of the campaign occurs before the Kick-off Event, so this chairperson must be ready to hit the ground running when the church council decides to go forward. This chairperson works very closely with the consultant and, as the Kick-off Event draws near, helps to announce the goal of the campaign.

> One parishioner wanted desperately to be part of the campaign leadership. He confided in me that he could only afford to give $25,000. While I thought this was a generous gift, it did not reach the level necessary to be the inspirational giver for the position of Advance Gift Chairperson. He stated that if I would help him get the position, he would write a check the next day for the full amount. This was his fatal mistake. As an experienced fund raiser, I felt that anyone who can write a check for $25,000 could give significantly more than that amount over five years. I challenged him to extend his gift over five years and to contribute $100,000. He started mentioning all the other people he knew who could more easily afford that. I convinced him that for him to ask another church member for $100,000, he would need to pledge that amount himself. I reminded him that he did not have to take the position. I also shared that I still needed to find someone to give at that level who could challenge others to do the same. Before we got up from lunch, he agreed to the $100,000 pledge. He then was able to confidently call on others who matched his generosity. He became a great advocate for the campaign and was heard to say over and over, "If not us, who? And if not now, when?"

The **Pattern Gift Chairperson's** role is to enlist other top leaders capable of soliciting gifts from prospects giving in an intermediate range. Pattern gifts will represent 30 to 35 percent of the goal. An inspirational gift must be made to the campaign. Like the Advance Gifts Chair, he will identify teams. Team captains and enough team members should be recruited to ensure that no team member has to solicit more than five to ten prospects. This person assures adequate orientation, training, and coaching of team members by the consultant prior to the selection of prospects. In coordination with the consultant, he oversees selection of prospects to help identify if another team member may be better suited to call on an individual. The team captain will solicit pledges from the team members.

The Spiritual Emphasis Chairperson's responsibilities include recruiting a small group of members who can assist with the various responsibilities of this committee. These responsibilities include preparing a prayer that can be used throughout the campaign such as during Sunday morning worship services, when groups meet during the week, and as a part of each family's daily devotions. He secures fifteen to twenty written testimonials from various church members. Statements may be about their reasons for endorsing the project, their personal stewardship decisions, or the importance of the church in their lives. He should plan a prayer vigil immediately prior to the Victory Team visitation phase and plan devotions of not more than three minutes for each steering committee meetings and the campaign training meetings. He works with the pastor to provide lay speakers (not more than three minutes) for worship services throughout campaign. This is an important position to keep the focus of the campaign on spiritual issues.

> A small Catholic church was having a difficult time recruiting someone to be the spiritual emphasis committee chair. A male parishioner had recently gone through a difficult divorce and had leaned heavily on the church to help him through it. The pastor, a very insightful man, had seen the man's great faith through his reliance on the church. The man had lost his footing in the community, and the pastor saw his involvement in the campaign as an opportunity. He invited this man to be the Spiritual Emphasis Chair. The man was deeply moved and embraced the job.

The Publicity Chairperson should ideally be someone who is familiar with public relations work. His responsibilities will include working with the Campaign Chairperson(s) and consultant in the preparation of all of the campaign materials, including fact sheets, as well as articles for the newsletter and bulletin. He coordinates all public announcements as to plans and progress reports concerning the campaign and prepares news releases as needed. This person also visits church organizations and Sunday school classes to communicate the aims, purposes, and goals of the campaign and creates the Capital Campaign goal chart.

The Kick-off Event Chairperson is responsible for the Kick-off Event, which will be discussed in detail in Chapter 8. The chairperson(s) will work closely with the Campaign Chairperson(s) and consultant to coordinate the event. Responsibilities include: recruiting a small committee such as a senior group to address invitations, selecting the menu, providing decorations, securing a speaker system and other visual aid equipment, and planning for nursery/childcare. This chairperson also arranges transportation for elderly and handicapped, forms a telephone committee to call each family, encourages attendance, recruits members of the steering committee and other officers of the church to serve as hosts/hostesses, and coordinates with the steering committee regarding the dinner program.

The Treasurer/Auditor certifies the consultant's record of pledges, deposits money as it is received, and keeps an accurate record of the total funds received and disbursed.

This person also coordinates the transfer of stocks, bonds, and other marketable assets, makes disbursements, and maintains a record of campaign expenses. It is also his responsibility to audit records and pledge cards at the end of the campaign and prepare a proper summary as required by the consultant and the steering committee.

Finance Committee: Depending on the size of the church, a finance committee may already exist. Or, an ad hoc committee might be established for the campaign, or the treasurer may be the finance committee. The committee must accomplish these things at all phases of the campaign:

- Approve the budget,
- Pay all bills,
- Monitor and audit all gifts made, including in-kind contributions, cash, and pledges,
- Provide an account, in writing, of the status and total of all pledges and amounts paid prior to the conclusion of the campaign.

Memorials Committee: This committee will identify naming opportunities and, with the assistance of the consultant and the Campaign Chairs, identify the gift level to be associated with each of these naming opportunities. It will also identify a means for recognizing memorial gifts and ensure that each memorial gift is recognized in the way the donor intended. Responsibilities include establishing a Memorials Book with appropriate and complete entries, writing "thank-you" letters for each memorial gift, and developing memorial gifts recognition in cooperation with the publicity committee. Your consultant can help you to determine what naming opportunities might be available and what level gift would be appropriate for these opportunities. Whether or not your church will accept naming opportunities or establish a memorial committee as part of the campaign, it is always appropriate to encourage gifts to be made in honor or recognition of someone.

The Materials of the Campaign

As with all things pertaining to the campaign, the materials must reflect the personality of your church. The View Book, the pledge card, the Visitor's Handbook, the campaign brochure, and the Kick-off Event program will be discussed in detail. All need to begin the design process as soon as the decision to move forward is made. Campaigns are short, and both design and printing take time.

The View Book: The View Book is a crucial way to send a clear and consistent message regarding the campaign. It is the Case for Support in a presentation format and serves as a script for the volunteers to follow when they make the visit. It is used during the Advance Gift Phase of the campaign. An experienced consultant will lay out in detail all of the text that should go into the View Book, including samples letters for the pastor and chairman, but the personality of the congregation must be reflected. All of the pages should be bound and easy to flip through. I always hear from creative design people that there should be a pocket in the back for all the included materials. I have found that this just makes a mess when you are trying to make the presentation. The View Book should be personalized for the person being called on. Since these are more expensive to prepare than the campaign brochure, they should be reserved for the most affluent and influential members of the church, approximately 10 percent of the congregation.

> I recently heard about an inexperienced consultant going on visits with a handful of church newsletters rather than a View Book. The campaign was not successful.

The View Book, and ultimately the brochure, should be designed with the understanding that it will be a clear and concise Case for Support. For the View Book to be used as a script for the visitors, I encourage the pages to be in the following order:

> Campaign prayer
> Mission statement
> Inspirational letter from the pastor
> Hearty endorsement from Campaign Chair
> History of the church
> Proposed new floor plans
> Site plan of the property
> Elevated rendering of the proposed new facilities
> Estimate of costs
> Memorial and naming opportunities if appropriate
> Capital Campaign vs. Annual Campaign differences (see below)
> Explanation of that gifts can be made over a three-to five-year period
> Listing of all of the church and campaign leaders

An excerpt from a View Book explains the difference between capital giving and annual pledging.

> Capital giving differs from annual pledging in several ways. Capital giving:
>
> - takes place only when absolutely necessary.
> - spreads out payments during a much longer period.
> - is in response to an urgent need.
> - seeks larger amounts than annual budgets can cover.
> - requires a planned, sacrificial, and inspirational effort, and often involves giving of real estate, securities, life insurance, or other tangible assets.
> - is over and above annual giving. Therefore, customary giving habits will not produce the desired results and assure a victory for your church's building campaign.

Some larger churches are now designing videos to spread the message. If done properly, this can be an extremely effective tool. I recently watched one for a church in Florida and it was so beautifully done that it brought a tear to my eye. The downside is that videos take a lot of time and money to do right. Videos do not replace personal visits, nor should the visit turn into watching the video together and then handing the person called on a pledge card. Some consulting firms push the development of a video. I don't think a video is going to make someone who otherwise wouldn't pledge do so. However, videos can be useful in particularly large individual churches or conference-wide/diocesan campaigns to help spread the word and create excitement for the project. Finally, if your church is engaged with outside counsel for your campaign, make certain that the firm pushing this on you doesn't own the video production company or have an agreement to be compensated for every church it convinces to do this.

The Pledge Card

An effective campaign program will have pledge cards personalized with the name and address of the family to be visited. This is the way we avoid duplication of campaign visits. It is extremely important that control is maintained over individual visits. Imagine what a waste of time it would be for different campaign visitors to be focused on trying to contact the same families. This could lead to the families feeling harassed. The database the campaign should use for the development of prospects is the entire mailing list. Many churches make the mistake of planning to ask only regular attending, or active, members to support the campaign. I have found that it is not only financially prudent to include all church members; it is also the moral and inclusive thing to do.

The pledge card should be printed on card stock with the emblem of the church and the theme of the campaign. The name of the family should either be printed on the card via a computer or attached via a sticker. Avoid handwriting the names on the cards; although it looks personalized, it also looks unprofessional.

The card should be able to fit in your pocket or purse and should have a perforated tear-off stub with the suggested level of giving. The stub is removed before the visit. The tear off is a reminder to the visitor of the suggested level of giving. It should be the size to fit in a jacket pocket or purse, because that is where it should stay during the presentation.

The card should include a description of the amount the family is pledging and of how the family intends to pay the pledge: via monthly or annual installations or in a lump sum. Some churches allow credit card and debit card payments, but there is usually a fee associated with those payments. The card should have a place for a signature. We have been adding a space on the back where someone can note if this gift is in memory or honor of someone.

A few years ago, one church insisted that the pledge card be oversized to stress the "importance" of the gifts to the campaign. Most ended up torn or tattered because they were oversized. In my experience, the size of the pledge card does not influence the size of the gift.

The Visitor's Handbook

This reference and practice guide has information about the consultant and leaders of the campaign as well as frequently asked questions with proposed answers. This book should be gone over in depth prior to making a visit. This should not be stapled looseleaf; it is best if it is bound so that it will not come apart.

The Campaign Brochure

The campaign brochure will contain all of the same essential elements of the View Book. The difference is that it can be mass-produced and will not be personalized. All members of the church who are not given a View Book will receive a campaign brochure. This brochure may or may not be distributed at the kick-off dinner. Like other aspects of the campaign, it needs to fit the personality of your congregation. The consultant needs to lay out the format and text of the brochure for the approval of the Campaign Steering Committee. While the brochure should be attractive, it should also be practical. Remember, the brochure, like the View Book, is to be used as a script for the visitors. It should be designed to present the needs in a clear and concise manner.

To maximize usefulness, I have found that the pages of the campaign brochure need to be in the following order:

Campaign prayer
Mission statement
Inspirational letter from the pastor
Hearty endorsement from Campaign Chair
History of the church
Floor plans
Site plan
Elevated rendering
Estimate of costs
Memorial and naming opportunities
Capital campaign versus annual giving (Figure 5)
Explanation that gifts can be made over a three-to five-year period
Listing of all of the church and campaign leaders

For an Episcopal Church campaign in Virginia, despite our pleading to the contrary, the Publicity Committee insisted in creating a brochure that was extremely elegant and quite beautiful. However, it contained no essential information regarding the campaign. In the back was a small pocket filled with the renderings of the proposed building and the cost estimates. Every time people opened the brochure, they were certain to lose a page or two from the back. Although the church was complimented on the appearance, the brochure became a sore point of the campaign due to the high cost and low functionality.

The Kick-off Event Program

A folded 8½x11-inch card stock page—with a picture of the church on the cover, the campaign prayer on the inside left, the program on the inside right, and perhaps the words to a closing hymn on the back cover—is a simple and effective way to set up the program. Use only one additional color to keep costs low.

> At a Catholic campaign Kick-off Event in Virginia, a bookmark-size piece of flimsy paper was distributed as people entered the event. This paper was to serve as the event program. The name of the church did not appear anywhere on the paper and there was more information regarding the entertainment that was being provided than on the campaign, the reason we were gathering. This was not ideal.

The Scale of Gifts

A good consulting firm will provide you with a Scale of Gifts necessary to achieve your needs. The scale is a listing of dollar amount in pledges that are required to reach a goal. In all of our campaigns, we strive to get a lead gift of 10 to 20 percent, and we have nearly always been successful in reaching that goal. Then there should be two gifts of 5 percent each of the goal. The next two to three gifts should be in the 2 to 3 percent range, and so on.

> At a Methodist church with less than 3,000 members, the leaders determined through their Focus Group Meetings that they had needs of $25 million. The campaign committee asked me to prepare a Scale of Gifts to see if they could in fact set $25 million as their goal. I prepared the Scale of Gifts and announced that the church would need a lead gift of $5 million and three $1 million gifts. The leaders balked at the amounts and complained that the congregation could not support that level of giving. I told them very matter of factly that that was fine; if they couldn't support that, they could readjust the plan. But I recommended that before they decided what the congregation couldn't do that they allow the congregation the chance to disappoint them. The leaders went forward with the requests, and every gift amount was met. At the Kick-off Event, they had over $12 million pledged and announced their goal of $25 million.

Typically, if you are trying to raise $5 million, a lead gift between $500,000 and $1 million is needed, followed by two $250,000 pledges, and ten $100,000 pledges. Remember that these amounts are being pledged over a three-to five-year period. Now you have to begin the sometimes contentious process of trying to identify who in the congregation should be called upon for these large gifts. I have found that there are two typical responses: churches that say that they have any number of people who could make those pledges and churches that say that no one can. I remind churches that this is a Scale of Gifts to meet these particular needs. If your congregation does not have people who can make these gifts, then we should readjust the expectations and make some decisions about which are the most urgent priorities.

The following illustrates a typical Scale of Gifts to raise $6 million:

SCALE OF GIFTS NEEDED TO RAISE $6 MILLION

ADVANCE GIFTS PHASE

Amount	No. of Gifts	No. of Prospects	To Raise $	Total $
$700,000	1	5	700,000	700,000
300,000	2	4	600,000	1,300,000
200,000	3	5	600,000	1,900,000
150,000	4	10	600,000	2,500,000
100,000	5	10	500,000	3,000,000

PHASE TOTAL $3,000,000

PATTERN GIFT PHASE

Amount	No. of Gifts	No. of Prospects	To Raise$	Total $
$75,000	10	20	750,000	750,000
50,000	15	30	750,000	1,500,000
35,000	20	40	700,000	2,200,000

PHASE TOTAL $2,200,000

VICTORY TEAMS PHASE

Amount	No. of Gifts	No. of Prospects	To Raise	Total $
$25,000	20	40	500,000	500,000
10,000	20	40	200,000	700,000
5,000	20	40	100,000	800,000

PHASE TOTAL $800,000

GRAND TOTAL $6,000,000

The Appraisals Process

A complete review process should be conducted to help determine what potential donors might consider contributing if they desired to make a commitment to the best of their ability. This can be a difficult process since no one really knows what anyone else's true ability is to contribute to a campaign. We need to encourage inspirational and sacrificial giving during a Capital Campaign. Therefore, persons must know what range of gift to "consider" to best help reach the goal. Only by presenting the request for gifts at specific levels can you succeed, because only by presenting target figures will you receive more than token contributions.

The "asking amount" is neither an assessment nor a requirement; it is a level of gift to consider that will help families and individuals make an educated decision regarding their gift. As visitors learn in our coaching sessions, "consider" is the key word in asking properly.

Every prospective donor or member of the church (family or individual) must be reviewed on an individual basis. Appraise prospects based on the level of gift they "could" give if they were 100 percent behind the project.

Be fair. Apply the golden rule: review or appraise each member of the church as you would like to be appraised. Targets should be a stretch, but not out of reach. If too many people make pledges over or at their asking amount, we have not challenged them to stretch in their giving.

Quite naturally, many people's first response to this approach is one of discomfort. In truth, presenting targets must be done in significant fund raising if there is to be any chance of reaching the goal. No campaign, whether for a hospital, school, or church, can reasonably expect to succeed without presenting to potential donors the targets that have been established in relation to the total needs.

In the context of an individual church campaign, we must first acknowledge that members are both financially capable and generous. However, a campaign effort still presents us with the challenge of having to raise the total funds necessary over three years with some asking to extend the payment period to five years. During a Capital Campaign, where asking amounts are presented, it will help to keep these principles in mind.

- We are stressing equal levels of sacrifice, not equal giving. All families have different circumstances. By asking families to consider gifts of various amounts, this reflects our sensitivity. Per capita giving is not productive for fund raising nor is it right to ask all families, regardless of their circumstances, to consider giving the same amount.

- Usually, our giving to any charitable or religious organization is based on what we want to give. The "asking amounts" established by developing a thoughtful and reasonable Scale of Gifts for your Capital Campaign and presented to the congregation by campaign visitors reflect what the church needs to fund the project.

- This "asking amount" is a figure that we are asking families to consider. It is not what you are supposed to give. It is not what you are expected to give. It is simply a target for you to consider.

- Because we usually need inspirational and sacrificial giving to reach our goal, some asking amounts will be more than some families can give. The main point is to stretch in your giving toward the target amount as much as possible.

Asking amounts in the campaigns my firm conducts are never derived by ZIP code, street name, or tax records. They should be arrived at by a small group of individuals who know the church family intimately and who can prayerfully and pastorally look at the scale and determine which families should be asked to consider various levels of gifts. Finally, it is of the utmost importance that in this process, all discussions and considerations are kept completely confidential. One of the reasons why this process is so successful is because of the respect shown to each family and because of the confidential nature of their gifts to the campaign.

> In a campaign at a Methodist church in Florida, the treasurer asked if it would be appropriate to do a financial review of everyone based on information on the Internet. I quickly stopped that line of discussion. You certainly do not want to be perceived by your members as having done background checks on them. This is a voluntary Christian process and should be kept that way.

Campaign Calendar

Once you have made the decision to move forward, your consultant should set up a campaign calendar. The consultant should be able to quickly tell you how many weeks you will need to personally meet with all of your families, because that is the true goal of the campaign, not the amount. One frequent problem I encounter is that some churches want to wait for the "perfect" time to do their campaign. The time of year is not important, even if you are a seasonal church with an ebb and flow of members. If you try to meet some artificial deadline to be inclusive of some members, you will lose other members' interest. Weather may determine the timing of your campaign, especially if you are a Northern church. It will be difficult for members to make face-to-face visits in January in that setting. If you intend to meet with every family individually, individual schedules can be accommodated. Don't worry too much about vacations and holidays in the campaign calendar; they can be worked around. In most cases, urgency of the project will determine the calendar.

Duration of the campaign. The length of the Capital Campaign, like the length of the Feasibility Study, will vary based on the size of the congregation. You want to allow enough time to ensure that every member of the congregation can be personally visited, but not to extend the effort so long that your volunteers burn out. The average campaign is ten to twenty weeks. Anyone who is involved in the campaign, especially the Campaign Steering Committee, will be expected to make the campaign effort a top priority. It is unreasonable to expect these individuals to make the effort a top priority if it is going to last a year or two. What is expected of them and the length of time to commit must be very clear. The length of the campaign, if conducted properly, has no bearing on the amount of money that can be raised. The method in which people are asked and the length of time needed to ensure all families are visited are all that drives the length of the campaign. A longer campaign only results in paying for a consultant for a longer period of time.

During a campaign in California, the chairman decided on his own to reduce the number of visiting weeks from ten to eight. I knew that the church could never finish visiting the congregation in eight weeks and that after our consultant left, no more visits would be conducted and the church would not reach its goal. I wanted the church to have a success, because I also wanted our firm to have a success. Since the chairman would not listen to me, I sent a letter to the steering committee congratulating the members on their Kick-off Event and reminding them that to reach their goal, they would need to schedule the full ten weeks. At the next campaign committee meeting, the members unanimously decided that the campaign effort would last ten weeks and requested that our consultant remained with them the full period. While the campaign was a bit difficult with a chairman being overruled, representatives ultimately were able to visit all members of the church and reached their goal.

Part of staying on track with the campaign calendar is ensuring that your volunteers know that they are the linchpins in your effort. Without their commitment to calling on the congregation, the task would be overwhelming for the campaign leadership. Volunteers are difficult to manage because you are not paying them to do a job; they are participating out of their commitment to the church. However, if volunteers are not making their calls in a timely manner or if they are not asking in the right way, you must stop them and either retrain them or simply thank them for their effort and find new volunteers. It is worse to have someone calling on people improperly than to have a delay in the calendar. When recruiting your volunteers, they should know that this is a real commitment.

Main Message

Those involved in the campaign are making a commitment that cannot be taken lightly. There is much to do; either you will do it all or you will recruit the right people to help. With a good consultant, identifying those people will be easier and will ultimately ensure the success of the campaign. The materials used in the campaign are nearly as important as the individual who personally delivers the message.

CHAPTER 6

The Right Way: How to Ask for Financial Support

> A Lutheran bishop had heard that an acquaintance in the synod had recently made a $500,000 commitment to a Methodist project. Surprised, the Lutheran bishop approached the acquaintance to ask if it was true. The individual had never given significantly to any of the Methodist programs. The man said it was true. When the bishop asked why he would give that money to a project outside the Lutheran church, the man replied, "Because they asked me."

You have determined through the Feasibility Study final report from your consultant that the congregation is in support of the ideas and spirit of the campaign. Now is the time you have to ask the members to prayerfully consider a gift. You personally engaged them for the Feasibility Study; now personally engage them in the Capital Campaign. Now is not the time to take short cuts. You should approach the members personally and in stages to manage the work load, but you must give all members the opportunity to be a part of the campaign at some point.

> My wife and I moved into a new church community and to our great surprise, on our second week, the pastor announced that they were in the midst of a $6 million Capital Campaign. I called the pastor to let him know that I had some experience in fund raising. He thanked me for the call and told me that the church had already engaged with outside counsel. I offered to assist in the campaign and gave him my contact information, which he assured me that he would pass along to the lay leadership. My wife, Molly, and I picked up a campaign brochure to familiarize

ourselves with the objectives of the campaign and began to prayerfully consider what we could contribute to the campaign, although we were not certain of the pledging period. Over the coming days and weeks, we continued to discuss what we could contribute and each time the amount was slightly increased. To our surprise, no one ever called to ask us to help make calls or to ask us for a pledge. We were shocked one Sunday at a church service when the pastor announced the end of the successful campaign. He announced that they had reached the goal of $3 million. He invited everyone who had not yet contributed to fill out pledge cards in the pews. Needless to say, we were very disappointed and did not feel that our contribution was either necessary or wanted. It is a lesson I pass along to every church I speak to. Our gift may not have been among the largest, but it would have been meaningful to us if we had been personally visited and asked for a pledge.

This chapter is dedicated to teaching you some of the key principles of asking for a gift. Some will tell you just to give a pledge card; others will encourage you to write a heart-wrenching letter of appeal. I will tell you that there has never been a letter written that is more effective than one member of a congregation calling on another member to request he prayerfully consider a gift to match one that the calling member has made. This is the area of my approach with which churches tend to be the most uncomfortable. The idea of asking each family for a gift can make them cringe, both at the work load and, more often, the idea of asking someone for a specific and large amount of money. I often explain it this way in campaign sales presentations: "How many of you in the room would be offended if someone you know from the church called and asked if he could come by to discuss the campaign?" No one has ever raised his/her hand. The key to these meetings is that the right person is chosen to ask the prospective campaign donor. It should be someone who has already made a pledge, someone who can articulate the plans of the campaign, and someone who knows the family being called upon.

After explaining to the committee the right way to make a call, a Campaign Chair decided to deviate from the path. He was due to call on a very prominent member of the community. He wanted to make the call because he wanted to bring in the lead gift and he was very confident this man would make it. At the committee meeting, we all waited to hear of his success. The chair arrived at the meeting and announced that instead of visiting the man, he sent him a letter with the View Book. My heart sank. I knew no good would come from this. I kept silent as the chair explained that he was certain he would get a very positive response. Before anyone could leave the room, I had to remind them that this was not the way to make the calls and I predicted that no pledge would come from the letter. The chair was angry with me. The following week he got a response to his letter. It was a terse reply stating that he had received it, would consider it, and was very surprised that a gift of this size would be addressed in a written request. Ultimately, the man made no pledge.

Administratively, there are only two essential elements to being a good volunteer:

1. Report on every card you agreed to take. If you don't see your prospects, no one else will.

> In one campaign, the chair decided that he would personally call on the largest six prospects. Two weeks into the campaign, he had not made any of his calls and few others had made theirs. I called the pastor and said that an emergency meeting was necessary. I gathered everyone and informed them that I was not interested in wasting their money and that I would leave if they were not going to make their calls. They all agreed to make their calls in the next week. As the week passed, I called the Campaign Chair, who had yet to make one of his calls. He gave me excuses and promised once again to make the calls. Before the telephone receiver was back on the hook I called him and told him that I needed to take back the pledge cards and materials he selected. He was shocked, but I was determined to get these six affluent members called on to give the campaign a jump start. I gave his pledge cards and materials to two other members who made the calls in the next few days. The campaign was a terrific success.

2. Work only from the pledge cards prepared by the office. This way we avoid duplication. If you want to call on a particular person, you should check with the office to make sure another visitor has not selected the prospect.

> In an Episcopal church campaign, a member of the congregation who was a stockbroker chose the pledge card of a wealthy church family. He had ulterior motives for wanting to meet this influential family. The visit got off track and the wealthy family member ended up declining to sign his pledge card. The stockbroker returned from the visit and announced that the wealthy family had no interest in the campaign. A short time later, the wealthy man's wife complained to the pastor that the stockbroker was trying to get her husband's business during the visit and that that was why they made no pledge. Another member of the Campaign Committee made a follow-up call. To our delight, she was welcomed to the home of the prospects and enjoyed a nice evening. The couple ended up pledging $50,000.

To make certain that a call is successful, use these **Ten Guiding Principles** for everyone in the campaign, from the pastor to a volunteer on any of the committees.

The Ten Guiding Principles

1. *Make your own gift first.* Give prayerful consideration to your own inspirational gift before visiting others. Then you can say, "Won't you join me?" You cannot sell others unless you have sold the campaign to yourself.

2. ***Use a team approach.*** Experience shows that teams get better attention, more serious consideration, and better results than individuals. Ensure that your partner has made a pledge to the campaign and be certain to practice the presentation together so that it is coordinated and not redundant.

3. ***Be informed.*** Understand the campaign objective and be able to articulate it through practicing before you go out on a call. The View Book or brochure gives you the needed information. Study them thoroughly and practice.

4. ***Be proud of your task and be yourself.*** You are providing friends with an opportunity to share with you and others in the future of your congregation. This is an investment in the future of the church, not a donation. Tell the story in your own style. Your conviction and enthusiasm will be the most important ingredient in your presentation. If the people were not able to attend the Kick-off Event, share some of the stories from the Kick-off with them.

5. ***Be committed.*** You need not be a professional salesperson to be a successful campaign visitor. Remember, you will be visiting friends who are interested in the future of your congregation. Delay and procrastination will only add to your anxiety of going on the first call and can slow down your momentum. One good gift, along with your own, will set the standard for others and boost your morale. Remember, every church member is important, and every gift necessary for success. *Never* try to solicit by telephone or by letter.

6. ***Ask for a specific gift.*** Seek a decision on the proper level. Begin at the high end of the range. It is next to impossible to begin at the lowest level and move up. Even if the gift is much less than the request, donors should feel good about what they can do, not sorry about what they can't do.

7. ***Be informed of various donation methods!*** Know that pledges may be made in cash, stocks, bonds, or other negotiable property. In addition, understand that pledges can be fulfilled over a period of time convenient to the donor.

8. ***Never, never leave the pledge card!*** If the church member wants to think about it, make an appointment to revisit but keep the card in your possession. People with the best intentions, myself included, can lose or misplace a pledge card. It can become uncomfortable to have to call the individual who visited you or the campaign office to say you are prepared to make a commitment, but can't find the pledge card. Follow up promptly and set a date for the answer and for the completion of the pledge card.

> In a recent campaign, the pastor and a consultant went to the home of an influential member of the congregation. The member had not yet decided on the amount he and his wife would pledge. He said to the pastor, "Leave the card and I will think about it." As the pastor was about to hand over the pledge card, despite his training to the contrary, the consultant found that he had inadvertently brought the wrong pledge card and apologized for the error. The member then asked what the next step was, and

the consultant said, "Prayerfully consider what you will give, and you can call me. I will take your word of your pledge and then send you a letter with the card."

When the pastor and consultant got out to the car, the pastor mentioned that it was fortunate that the consultant had brought the wrong card. The consultant stated, "Pastor, after you left cards at the last two visits, I wasn't about to let you do it a third time."

The pastor was a little angry that the consultant had intentionally brought the wrong card; however, when the pledges came in for the three visits, the two who had the pledge cards left at their home gave significantly less than the member who called the consultant to share his prayerfully considered gift amount.

9. **Complete the pledge card.** Assist the prospect in filling out the card. Be certain the total amount is indicated, the payment plan noted, and the donor signs the card.
10. **Thank the donor for his or her time!** All gifts are welcome and are accepted graciously, no matter the size. Also, be sure to thank the church member for his time even if he decides not to make a gift.

In an Episcopal campaign project in Minnesota, the rector made a visit to an elderly family. The couple pledged $50,000, but the rector did not have them formally sign the pledge card. Later that evening, the man unexpectedly died leaving the widow to decide if she could now honor the pledge they had made together even though they had not signed the card. She did.

Asking for the Pledge

How exactly do you ask for a gift? Many individual donors ask, "What do you expect from me?" or "What are others giving?" There should be no embarrassment in mentioning a specific amount you want them to consider if you have thought about it beforehand. You may anonymously report what others have pledged, or report the average gift. Let the person know that others are responding generously. You compliment, not offend, by suggesting a specific and substantial amount for someone to prayerfully consider.

A tactful and honest way of suggesting an amount is to say, "For us to reach our goal, each of us must give a considered gift according to our commitment, interest, and financial situation. We are hopeful that you will be among those subscribing $ _____ per month for three or five years. You may have it in mind to give more, or you may not feel you cannot give so much. If you find it possible to consider this amount, your commitment at this time will help us be successful." Tell the prospective donor, "Whatever you decide to give, after prayerful consideration and thinking the matter over in the light of the campaign goal and your other obligations, will be appreciated." Experience has shown that most people appreciate such an honest and forthright approach. This is not a new idea. The following is a speech given by John D. Rockefeller, Jr in 1933 to the Citizen Family Welfare Committee of New York City.

"I have been asked to say a few words on the techniques of soliciting donations.

Perhaps the best way to acquire knowledge of that subject is to ask ourselves the question, "How would I like to be approached for a gift?" The answer, if carefully thought out, may be relied upon as a pretty safe guide to the task of soliciting. I have been brought up to believe, and the conviction only grows on me, that giving ought to be entered into in just the same careful way as investing—that giving is investing, and that it should be tested by the same intelligent standards. Whether we expect dividends in dollars or in human betterment, we need to be sure that the gift or the investment is a wise one and therefore we should know all about it. By the same token, if we are going to other people to interest them in giving to a particular enterprise, we must be able to give them adequate information in regard to it, such information as we would want were we considering a gift.

First of all, then, a solicitor must be well informed in regard to the salient facts about the enterprise for which he is soliciting. Just what is its significance, its importance? How sound is the organization in back of it, how well organized? How great is the need? An accurate knowledge of these and similar facts is necessary in order that the solicitor may be able to speak with conviction.

It is a great help to know something about the person whom you are approaching. You cannot deal successfully with all people the same way. Therefore, it is desirable to find out something about the person you are going to—what are his interests, whether you have any friends in common, whether he gave last year, if so how much he gave, what he might be able to give this year, etc. Information such as that puts you more closely in touch with him and makes the approach easier.

Again, one always likes to know what other people are giving. That may be an irrelevant question, but it is an asked question. If I am asked for a contribution, naturally and properly I am influenced in deciding how much I should give by what others are doing.

Another suggestion I like to have made me by a solicitor is how much it is hoped I will give. Of course, such a suggestion can be made in a way that might be most annoying. I do not like to have anyone tell me what it is my duty to give. There is just one man who is going to decide that question—who has the responsibility of deciding it—and that is myself. But I do like a man to say to me, "We are trying to raise $4,000,000 and are hoping you may be desirous of giving blank dollars. If you see your way clear to do so, it will be an enormous help and encouragement. You may have it in mind to give more; if so, we shall be glad. On the other hand, you may feel you cannot give as much in view of other responsibilities. If that is the case, we shall understand. Whatever you give after thinking the matter over carefully in the light of the need, your other obligations, and your desire to do your full share as a citizen, will be gratefully received and deeply appreciated." When you talk to a man like that he is glad to meet you again and will not take the other elevator when he sees you in the corridor because you backed him to the wall and forced him to give.

Of supreme importance is it to make a pleasant, friendly contact with the prospective giver. Some people have a less keen sense of their duty and responsibility than others. With them, a little urging may be helpful. But with most people, a convincing presentation of the facts and the need is far more effective. When a solicitor comes to you and lays on your heart the responsibility that rests so heavily on his; when his earnestness gives convincing evidence of how seriously interested he is; when he makes it clear that he knows you are no less anxious to do your duty in the matter than he is, that you are just as conscientious, that he feels sure all you need is realize the importance of the enterprise, and if so, how much, it is for him alone to decide.

To recap then, briefly: know your subject; be so sold on it yourself that you can convincingly present its claims in the fewest possible words. A letter may well precede an interview, but personal contact is the most effective. Know as much as you can about the man to whom you go; give him a general idea as to the contributions being made by others in his group, and suggest in a gracious and tactful way what you would be glad to have him give, leaving it solely to him to decide what he shall give. Be kindly and considerate. Thus will you get closest to a man's heart and his pocketbook."

A Capital Campaign victory can be lost by . . .

- indifference
- procrastination
- the use of letters, telephone calls, or chance meetings rather than planned and scheduled personal visits
- thinking that "our church's circumstances are different" as a basis for circumventing proven campaign methods
- a failure to see the value of the campaign
- a failure to become aligned with the vision, or a tendency toward disinterestedness
- a failure to develop a belief in the ultimate achievability of the objectives

A Capital Campaign victory can be achieved by . . .

- seeing that all church members attend the kick-off celebration
- strict adherence to the time schedule
- advance visits with church leaders, other influential members, and those members who have more resources and are capable of larger gifts
- a well-organized, informed, and enthusiastic group of visitors
- personal visits with every member of the church
- regular Report Meetings attended by each visitor

- the recognition that capital needs are different from annual pledging and require a prayerful and inspirational effort on the part of each member of the congregation, leader and follower alike

In the chapters that follow, each of the following phases of the campaign will be detailed: the Advance Gift Phase, the Kick-off Event, the Pattern Gift Phase, and the Victory Team Phase.

MAIN MESSAGE

Personal visitation creates and enhances Christian Stewardship. Treat people with honesty and respect. Let them know what is required to reach a particular goal. Also, always ask an individual in person for a specific gift.

CHAPTER 7

Campaign Phase I: Advance Gifts

> A church elder once told me, "I learned a long time ago not to decide what others are not going to do." That statement has stayed with me and has given me the strength to ask people for things that otherwise I might not.

All phases of the campaign are critical; however, this phase is going to be predictive of what you are going to raise in the entire Capital Campaign. This should also be known as the Goal Confirmation Phase. It is conducted quietly by the Campaign Steering Committee (Executive Committee), authorized by the church leaders. This is a nonpublic period of the campaign that occurs prior to the Kick-off Event. What you raise during this phase is typically 50 percent of what you are going to raise in the total campaign. Even though you may have needs of $10 million, if you only raise $3 million in this phase, announce a goal of $6 million. Some firms call this the challenge gift phase. We don't prescribe to this terminology only because we believe in equal sacrifice, not equal giving, so that all gifts are equally challenging regardless of the phase.

The beginning of the Advance Gift Phase should not begin with an official campaign goal but should begin with campaign needs. This is very important distinction for people to understand. The needs were established in the Case Statement. You may not be able to raise this, and therefore it should not be your stated goal. Until you see what is raised in the advance gifts phase, do not set a goal.

Now is the time to begin asking, using the format discussed in the last chapter. Begin with those closest to the campaign. The campaign leadership was selected based on their need to make an inspirational gift; now, beginning with the pastor, they should be called upon to make their pledge. All of the campaign leadership should have their pledges made before they begin asking anyone else to make pledges. After the campaign leaders are called upon, your consultant should help you to identify other "perceived" leaders in the congregation. Typically, 10 to 15 percent of the members will be visited during this Advance Gifts Phase. Starting with those closest to the campaign and then expanding the circle from there is the most effective method. This goes against the teachings of most other fund raisers who will want you to target the wealthiest first. However, establishing that the leaders are taking an interest will generate enthusiasm in the campaign and make it easier for those leaders to recruit others to their committees.

Quality giving will be emphasized during this early period, since the pattern of giving set at this stage will influence all other gifts secured in the campaign.

> A bishop involved in a Methodist campaign for $5 million told me that there was no one in the conference that could give a lead gift of 10 percent. I argued that someone must have the ability over a five-year period, and he fought about giving me a name. Finally, I asked who the wealthiest Methodist in the conference was, and he gave a name. The meeting was arranged and I told him that even if he was right that this person did not have the ability, he needed to ask so the campaign could be a success. The bishop was so nervous going into the meeting, thinking he was going to insult this very wealthy man. After a few minutes into the meeting, he blurted out that he really needed a $500,000 gift to make the campaign a success. The businessman thought for a moment and said, "Bishop, I would be honored to make that pledge." The bishop was stunned, but left the meeting as the biggest advocate of at least asking.

Progress will be evaluated frequently, at least weekly, including a measurement of readiness of response, spirit of endorsement, level of cooperation, and actual commitments of top gifts. This report should come from the consultant, due to the confidential nature of contributions.

At the conclusion of the Advance Gifts Phase, progress toward your goal will be appraised, and all options are open to you. The steering committee will confirm the official campaign goal or, if necessary, adjust the objective to the appropriate level. Once established and confirmed, the goal will be presented to the entire church at the Kick-off Event.

When a congregation strives to achieve a common goal and meets it, that is as important as the monies that are raised. In twenty years, the congregation might not remember how much was raised or for what the money was used, but the members will most likely remember if they had a successful campaign.

The amount pledged during the Advance Gifts Phase provides the basis of the campaign objective that is announced at the Kick-off Event. The event itself is fun and shares information. All members are encouraged to attend and no solicitations of gifts take place.

Naming Opportunities

At a campaign in Maryland, in the midst of a $4 million campaign in which six classrooms were proposed to be added to the parish hall, the building committee chair proposed that each classroom naming opportunity should have a $25,000 gift associated. Given the Scale of Gifts needed to reach the goal, I suggested that perhaps a $100,000 gift tag be associated. She resisted until I convinced her that not only did we need the higher Scale of Gifts to hit the goal, but that there were going to be many people in the church who could give $5,000 a year for five years. Unless we were going to give all of those people a naming opportunity, it would not be fair and could cause hard feelings.

I am often asked what my thoughts are with respect to memorial gifts and naming opportunities. I feel that memorial gifts, donations made in memory or gratitude of someone such as a loved one who has passed, are a wonderful way to contribute to anything. Whether it is a gift to the church building fund, the community hospital, Boys and Girls Club, or local library, all are worthy causes and will recognize a gift made in memory of someone. I believe that naming opportunities for a church campaign must fit with the personality of the congregation. I have visited some churches that have a name on everything from windows to the janitor's closet. Still, many churches resist recognizing donors altogether in the form of brass plates or plaques. Naming opportunities have encouraged many, many people to contribute vast amounts of money. I certainly would not rule it out. However, I do have some advice when the decision is made to offer naming opportunities. Make sure there are enough opportunities for a large number of families. If you will allow someone's name on a room, make certain you allow this for all rooms, not just some of the classrooms. Opportunities for the conference rooms, pastor's study, parlor, library, and other rooms can be very appealing. When your naming opportunities are limited, you must set the dollar amounts high.

During a project several years ago with a United Methodist church, I was working with a pastor so dedicated to the cause and consumed by the success of his parish that he made the building of a new parish hall one of the most important objectives in his career. He felt he was called at this place in time to provide for the future generations of this church. During a campaign visit with a successful businessman, the pastor and I asked him to prayerfully consider being the lead gift donor of $1 million. This lead gift would certainly ensure a successful campaign and with it, the naming opportunity of the new parish hall. The prospective donor contemplated his gift and confessed that he truly felt that he was blessed by God with these resources. He explained that these resources really belonged to God and that he was merely entrusted to be a good steward. This heartfelt and emotional meeting ended with this wonderful man accepting the challenge for the lead gift of $1 million. However, he declined the naming opportunity. He said it would not be appropriate to put his name on the new facility. I felt that I was in the presence of a great man. How could this get any better? Several months later, after the campaign had come to a very successful end, a ground-breaking ceremony was arranged. At that time, it was announced that the lead gift donor had ultimately accepted the naming opportunity. It was his wish to name the new parish hall after the pastor who worked tirelessly to make the campaign a success. I still get tears in my eyes when I think of that day.

Some churches want to set a goal shortly after the first few gifts are in. Our recommendation is to wait until the last minute before the Kick-off Event to decide on the goal, based on what has been pledged to date. This encourages everyone to continue working down to the last minute. If the goal is set too early, people tend to slow down.

MAIN MESSAGE

Set an official campaign goal only after key leaders and largest potential donors make their financial commitments to the total cost of the project. It is important for these donors to make commitments based on actual needs rather than an arbitrary goal. Also, use naming opportunities only if this fits with the personality of your church.

CHAPTER 8

The Kick-off Event

A man and his wife arrived at the church's Kick-off Event. While they had not discussed the campaign, both fully expected to be asked for a pledge before the end of the evening even though the invitation stated that there would be no solicitation of funds. As they sat down, the man leaned over to his wife and confided that they could contribute $10,000 when the pledge cards were distributed. She agreed. As they listened to all of the heartfelt testimonials about the importance of the needs, he then leaned over and said, "When they pass out the pledge cards, we can do $25,000," and she agreed. The blessing was given and the members dispersed and they drove home, amazed at the event. When the campaign volunteer met with the couple a few days later, she said that since the Kick-off Event, they had done a lot of prayerful consideration and ultimately committed to a $100,000 pledge.

Every time I hear a story such as this, it reinforces to me that the Kick-off Event is not the venue in which to ask people for their gift. There are two reasons. Some people get so moved by the testimonials that they may commit to a gift that they cannot afford, or feel pressured in a setting where everyone around them is signing a pledge card. The second reason is that others will not put much thought into their gift and choose a token amount without being truly challenged. In a group setting, you certainly don't want tables deciding among themselves what the average gift should be.

So, if we are not asking for pledges at the event, what is the point? There are three objectives to the Kick-off Event. The first is to educate the members about the Feasibility Study and what was decided regarding the needs and the proposed solutions. To do this, it is important to provide a clear Case Statement, developed from the results of the Feasibility Study and delivered by the Campaign Chair. The second is to introduce and recognize all of those members who are involved in the campaign. The third is to announce how much money has been pledged. If a goal has been set, that should also be announced at that time. If you decide to announce the goal at the event, you should have at least half of the goal pledged.

> Many years ago, my wife and I were invited to a Catholic church Kick-off Event. It was a church with which she had worshipped many years earlier and felt a personal connection. We had driven in from out of town to attend. Since it was a late afternoon event and the location was a beautiful downtown hotel, I made the assumption that this would be a sit-down dinner. Neither of us had eaten, and when we arrived, we found a small hors d'oeuvres table set up in one corner and an open bar in another corner. We were told that we were each welcome to eat five hors d'oeuvres and have two drinks. We could not bring ourselves to take a seat, given the advanced age of the average attendee and the lack of chairs. No explanation was made as to why we were all gathered, other than the church needed to expand. Renderings of the proposed buildings were hidden in a corner. Musical entertainment interrupted the program and broke the rhythm of the testimonials. The people chosen to speak on behalf of the program did not effectively make the case and certainly were not practiced. We left the event wondering what the needs truly were as we were never told explicitly. At dinner, later that night, instead of discussing the needs of the church and how we would support them, we focused on how poorly the message of the campaign was delivered. We were certain that no one in attendance took away any more from the event than we did. This only reinforced in my mind what is necessary for an effective Capital Campaign Kick-off Event.

We have been involved in a number of venues for Kick-off Events, from elaborate country club events to modest fellowship hall buffets. Regardless of the location, the event needs to build community and reflect the personality of the church. I have always been a strong advocate of a sit-down meal with an organized program. A relaxed atmosphere and the ability to socialize with eight to ten people at a table can go a long way toward building enthusiasm for a project. I have found it helpful if the members of the church are not directly involved in serving the food and cleaning up, as they should be included in the event and paying attention to the guests.

The purpose of the Kick-off Event is to educate and inspire, and to celebrate what has been accomplished thus far.

This is one of the most important elements of the entire Plan of Campaign. Most Kick-off events revolve around a dinner; however, many of our church clients, in keeping with their personality, have had some other event such as a brunch or barbecue as the setting. All that matters is that the venue must be able to accommodate all members, be free of charge to encourage participation, and have an adequate sound system to get the news of the campaign delivered.

It is important to mail out an invitation with the RSVP card several weeks in advance of the event. It is most appropriate when the invitation is hand-addressed and is stamped with first-class postage. A considerate church and campaign committee will ensure the RSVP cards are stamped. It is important to make responding as easy as possible for the invited guests. Even under the best circumstances, a great deal of advertising and follow-up are necessary to get the desired attendance. In most cases, the church will advertise the event in the Sunday bulletin and the church newsletter, and announce it in services. In addition, most churches today have the ability to use the Internet to announce the event. In some cases, it is important to recruit a telephone committee to follow up on the mailing to encourage all members to attend.

The invitation should resemble a formal invitation and should include the event date, location, purpose, keynote speaker, and the fact that there will be no solicitation of funds. A church that desires a successful Campaign Kick-off Event will do everything in its power to get the greatest number of members to attend.

Your Kick-off Event Committee Chair has now recruited his committee and they have been very busy planning for the event. Things they have considered included the venue, the time of day, the menu, the anticipated attendance, recruiting a keynote speaker if desired, the availability of or need for childcare during the event, transportation for those who otherwise wouldn't drive or attend a function at the time of day chosen, parking, name tags, event brochures . . . just to name a few.

The Kick-off Event program is essential. The program lets everyone knows what to expect and when to expect it.

> Opening prayer
> Dinner (forty minutes) or other social time
> Presentation of the overview/purpose of the campaign
> Acknowledgment of volunteers
> Testimonials
> Introduction of the keynote speaker
> Progress of Campaign
> Announce the Campaign goal
> Inspirational words by Pastor
> Hymn
> Closing prayer

Keep the event on time and timely. It should not last more than two hours; after that, you begin to lose people. You want them to leave feeling inspired, not drained.

The program, similar to the Feasibility Study program presentation, should give a brief presentation on the campaign's total needs. In addition, it's important to walk through the plans and the scope of the project. All church members who have agreed to take on leadership roles in the campaign should be recognized. Throughout the program, it is important to have testimonials given by various church members. These testimonials are essentially endorsements of the proposed plans with a personal emphasis. The people selected to give these testimonials should be a good cross-section of the congregation.

Some churches will have entertainment before or after the presentation or during dinner. A few points to consider:

Let the church members write their own names on name tags. This way they will be called by the name of their choosing. Also, if you preprint all of the nametags and there is poor turnout, the absence of the other members will be obvious from the sea of name tags on the welcome table.

If you decide to have a keynote speaker, remember that his/her job is to inspire and to act as a draw for attendance. This may be a popular bishop, a pastor of a neighboring church that has gone through the same program, or a popular local celebrity.

For those churches that are trying to raise money for a fellowship hall, it is often helpful to the cause to hold the event in a local church fellowship hall that is similar to the one you are trying to build. It will contribute to the vision.

> During one Kick-off Event for a United Methodist church at a restaurant, one of the leaders of a campaign brought out a tape measure during dinner and ran it a third of the way through the audience. She then announced that what she had just measured off was the size of the current fellowship hall. She then pointed to all those sitting beyond the mark and announced that if the event had been held in the current hall, none of them could have attended. It drove home the need to expand the facility. It was very effective.

If you can in some way incorporate an event at the Kick-off Event that involves children of the parish, it will ensure that their parents will attend. The downside is that the parents may be distracted from the rest of the event.

There are opposing views on the timing for distributing the campaign brochure, described in Chapter 5. Some will argue not to give out the brochure during the Kick-off Event, because people will be focused on reading it and will not pay attention to the program. Others say that the brochure can be given as people leave the event. Still others argue that the delivery of the brochure can provide a reason for the personal visits later.

I have seen the brochure passed out at the Kick-off Event and I have seen cases where the brochure is given out at the personal visit. Neither method has cost a campaign success or ensured a victory. However, it is always important that the campaign fits the personality of the congregation and leaders of the effort.

Main Message

The purpose of the Kick-off Event is to educate and inspire all members of the congregation.
It is not a time to ask for pledges. Do not charge for the event.
Often, a campaign Kick-off Event is the only time the entire congregation gets together for one individual event. Therefore, make it enjoyable and memorable.

CHAPTER 9

Campaign Phase 2 and 3:

Pattern Gifts and Victory Teams

The Kick-off Event is complete and the congregation knows that you are well on your way to achieving your goal. You have reached what is officially considered the start of the campaign's public phase. You should have half or more of your goal pledged prior to the Kick-off Event, so now you are targeting to raise the other half of the goal. This will be done in two parts. The first is called the Pattern Gifts Phase; the second is the Victory Teams Phase. Both have similar administrative responsibilities. They differ primarily in terms of size of the volunteer effort and the asking amounts. In the Pattern Gifts Phase, you are still targeting some of the larger gifts; in the Victory Team Phase, you are going after everyone not yet called upon.

Pattern Gifts: The financial goal of this phase is to raise 30 percent of the total. Members to be visited during this phase were identified during the breakout of the Scale of Gifts. The average pledge requested will vary based on your goal. The campaign visitors for this phase should be ready to go once the Kick-off Event ends. That means that they should all be called on for their pledge and trained just prior to the Kick-off Event. No one should become a visitor without having been called on by someone who has already been trained and who has made a pledge. Once someone is asked and makes his pledge, he is eligible to become a visitor. While there is a lot of potential in this phase, there is also a lot of room for sloppy behavior and mistakes to be made. Having a consultant present to oversee the training and debrief the callers is essential. Breaking bad habits early is also essential.

The true value of the Feasibility Study is realized in the implementation of this phase. During the study, many people noted on their questionnaires that they would be willing to participate. Imagine how difficult it would be if you were cold calling everyone in the parish, and having to give them a mini Feasibility Study to assess their willingness to help.

The Pattern Gift Chair reports and meets as needed with the consultant, who continues to oversee training of volunteers. The Pattern Gift Chair reports weekly to the Campaign Chair and the pastor.

The number of visitors will be relatively small, but their responsibility is great. All members of the congregation will be treated in the same, respectful manner, using the "ask" technique described in Chapter 6. Orientation and coaching sessions will be conducted for all who accept the invitation to become visitors. An initial orientation meeting, which includes the first coaching session (we coach volunteers constantly throughout the campaign) and pledge card selection, will be followed by regular Report Meetings. Pledge card selection is an important element in an effective and successful effort. It is more important to allow campaign visitors to select on whom they wish to call rather than to assign cards to them. Campaigns directed by my firm give visitors the option of the number of visits they wish to make and the individuals or families to visit. When I hear of campaigns directed by other firms that assign pledge cards based on geographic area or some other means, I wonder why they don't let the visitors make the decisions. Many campaign volunteers, while excited about a building project, can also be reluctant to make visits for fear or rejection or some other concern. Make it as easy as possible for those volunteers who are giving of their time to make the campaign effort a success. Allow them to decide whom they will visit.

Also completed during this time is the recruitment and training for the final phase of solicitation, the Victory Teams.

Victory Teams: The financial aim of this phase is to raise the final 20 percent of the campaign goal. This is an intense period of the campaign because the most visitors will be trained during this phase in order to reach out to all of the members of the congregation who have not yet been visited. To accomplish this, accurate membership records are a necessity.

Our consultant will provide a brief weekly report to all appropriate leaders, as well as our office.

Toward the end of a campaign, when the committee members are tired, it is sometimes necessary to use extraordinary means to get the volunteers to refocus their efforts.

> In one of my very first campaigns, as we neared the end of the ten-week campaign we were approximately $10,000 short of our goal. With the bishop preparing to visit on Victory Sunday and the number of calls dwindling, I addressed the slowdown with the committee. At one of our last meetings, I wrote a memo prepared for the Campaign Steering Committee members' signatures that promised that if they did not raise the money by a certain date, they would collectively contribute the additional funds. Without exception, they all reluctantly signed the letter. The Finance Chair astutely said, "This is just our consultant's way of telling us to keep our eye on the ball and get our calls done." Within days, the goal was reached, and I received an envelope with the torn-up memo. I was very pleased.

If new members join the church during either of these phases, they should be approached not because you are desperate, but because they have joined the church and deserve be treated like all of the other members. Some church members may not want to offend them by asking for money just as they join. In my experience, asking them to become a part of the future of the church by making a contribution to the campaign will include them, not offend them.

> In an Episcopal project in Arkansas, a widow had recently joined the church. Some members did not want to approach her for a pledge for fear of offending her due to her short tenure with the parish. Since we were still in the midst of the project, I encouraged them to approach her. We argued over the asking amount since no one knew her well. It was decided that she would be asked to consider a pledge of $25,000. The pledge card was made up and the Campaign Chairman prepped for the visit. When he arrived, he was pleased with her enthusiasm for the campaign and the fact that she was happy to be a part of the future of the church. During their visit together, she shared a great deal of information with him regarding her very positive financial situation. It was obvious she had great means and could consider a gift greater than $25,000. After the visit, the chairman called me to report that he respectfully asked her to consider a gift of $75,000, which she cheerfully pledged.

Victory Celebration

The Victory Celebration is an especially important event. It says "thank you" in a memorable way and marks the completion of the more active phase of the campaign. The Victory Celebration may not directly correlate with the departure of your consultant, especially if significant outstanding calls remain. The celebration should take place in anticipation of reaching of the pledge goal. Some churches invite the surrounding community to the event, as they know their future building plans will be an inconvenience to the community. It might otherwise be coupled with an upcoming event in the church's history such as a twenty-five-year celebration. As with all aspects of the campaign, it must reflect the personality of the church. It should be organized similar to the Kick-off Event with attention to recognizing the hard work that went into the campaign.

Main Message

You will be able to readily identify your workers for the Pattern Gifts and Victory Teams phases of the campaign if you have done your Feasibility Study correctly.
Follow-through in these phases is the key to the ultimate success of the campaign.
Recognition of the hard work done throughout the campaign is needed to boost morale and motivate those who will need to continue to monitor the campaign.

CHAPTER 10

Follow-through: Keeping the Campaign Alive

At the conclusion of our contracted resident service, all records and documents pertaining to the campaign belong to your church and are left for your reference and records. Based upon past experience, our Director will design an effective collection and follow-up program. These plans will assure minimum pledge loss and will maintain interest and support of the many members who worked on and contributed to the campaign. We maintain intermittent contact with leaders of your church throughout the pledge payment period.

There are two main objectives of this period. One is to keep the campaign in front of the congregation as a reminder that it is still going on while they continue to pay on their pledges. The second is to visit new members to the church to gain their support for the project.

I am often asked how much of the actual pledges are paid over the five-year period, and I always remark that just as with the rest of the campaign, that is up to you. Historically, approximately 96 percent of pledges are paid. What we are seeing now is that churches that have an excellent Follow-up Committee can actually see a substantial increase in pledges by continuing to approach new members and call on them to join in the campaign.

> At a Methodist church in Maryland two years after the official campaign had ended, a young couple joined the church and the Follow-up Committee called on them regarding the campaign. Although they were new members, they felt that the project was very worthwhile and they had seen the transformation of the church, which is why they had joined. They pledged $250,000.

Follow through works when there is a committed team assigned to the committee. No program will sustain its momentum for thirty-six to sixty months without constant assistance. Your job is to keep it alive and well over the course of the commitment period. The Follow-up Committee should meet at least once a quarter. The initial suggestion is to pick the first week of each third month. The publicity representative needs to meet with the campaign treasurer and church secretary on at least a monthly basis to gather information that can be used in the newsletter, updates, and special mailings.

To have the most effective Follow-Up Program:

1. Appoint a small ad hoc committee of three to five dedicated individuals who have displayed leadership during the course of the campaign to oversee the follow-through on pledge payments.

2. Keep all campaign records, collection procedures, and accounts completely separate from other expense and income records.

3. Treat all gifts, payments, and records confidentially.

4. Have the financial secretary keep a record of pledge payments and send reminders to donors one month before their payments are due. This person should also provide a list of delinquent payments for the follow-through task force.

5. Keep accurate records of giving, and use money only for the purposes listed in the campaign.

6. Make positive announcements to keep members and friends of the church informed and encouraged.

7. Write positive and personal thank-you letters. Never write negative or pressure-type letters.

8. Enlist new donors through personal visitation.

9. Some contributors have made one-year or cash gifts. Often, these persons will consider additional gifts in subsequent years if approached properly and in person.

Some helpful things to keep the campaign alive:

1. Newsletters and Updates

At the end of each three-month period, mail an informative letter, update, or newsletter to donors, stating the results of pledging and the campaign progress to date. Explain plans for the future. Communication is one of the most effective means of maintaining momentum. When major projects are completed, try to obtain coverage from both the diocese or conference and local media outlets.

2. Frequent Announcements

Make frequent announcements to those who participate in the various ministries conducted at your church. Remember that people are drawn to churches that are vibrant and alive, where *worthwhile things are really happening*. Make sure that visitors are made aware that the church has recently undertaken a *successful* campaign. Announce when important milestones have been reached.

In Case of Delinquent Payments

Each case should be handled based on its own circumstances. If a personal call becomes necessary, the approach should be as one friend who is interested in helping another solve a situation. Do not use the mail except for quarterly or annual statements. Always phone or go in person to avoid any misunderstandings.

In the rare case that it becomes obvious there is no hope of redeeming the pledge, offer to reduce or otherwise revise the amount. If this does not solve the problem, offer to recommend to the committee that the pledge be canceled. It is useless to keep harassing someone who cannot or will not fulfill his obligation. It will only cause hard feelings, and that was not the spirit in which the campaign was conducted.

Negativism must not be allowed to detract from a general tone of optimism, sincerity, and urgency. If you as leaders reflect any doubts or misgivings about the good faith of those who have pledged, you will adversely affect collections. As you constantly confirm the conviction that the program will proceed as planned, based on faith in the pledges and the vitality of the pledges, you will strengthen all concerned. Each pledge should be regarded as a sacred and solemn commitment—a commitment upon which you are building.

Helpful Tools

Match the computer records of pledges to the original, signed pledge cards to make certain they are accurate. Some backup disks should be kept off-site so that in the event of an emergency, a copy of the pledge information will always remain safe.

Sample kits containing all materials should be left in the office. The kits contain the names of the persons who demonstrated leadership of one kind or another during the campaign. As time passes, you will find it interesting to see how the church progressed and reached a successful conclusion. The Plan of Campaign will always be a good resource to consider for any future campaigns.

Nominations for Campaign Follow-up Committee
Duties: Publicity, monitoring of pledges, following up delinquencies, financial projections and tracking, and convening.

NAME	*RESPONSIBILITY*
_____	*Publicity*
_____	*Follow-up/Treasurer*
_____	*Presentation/Newcomers*
_____	*Presentation/New Members*
_____	*Presentation/ New Members*
_____	*Presentation/New Members*
_____	*Handling Delinquencies*
_____	*Handling Delinquencies*
_____	*Convener*

Main Message

Keep the campaign in front of the congregation and show them progress. Campaign follow-up procedures are necessary, and the volunteers who serve on this committee have a great responsibility to keep the campaign alive.

CHAPTER 11

Combining Annual with Capital Campaigns

Many churches over the past several years have approached me about the possibility of combining the Annual Campaign with a Capital Campaign. While the practice once was considered forbidden in fund-raising circles, my firm has managed to establish a track record of success in combining the efforts. The key is clearly delineating the objectives of each program and then educating the congregation regarding the ministry of each. The advantage to combining these efforts is that there is decreased stress on your volunteers, and communication regarding the objectives of each can be more clearly defined.

Often, members of the church are confused about the difference of each effort. We hear members remark during most Capital Campaigns, "Didn't we just make a pledge to the church last year?" Members can become confused over the difference between annual ministries, which include elements of the annual budget, and capital needs such as new construction, renovation, or property acquisition, etc.

Capital Campaigns usually invest in permanent properties and are usually so significant that the annual budget of the church could not possibly address these costs. I have found that some members understand the difference very well. Often, we see church members with low annual giving surprise many in the congregation by pledging large sums of money when a naming opportunity is presented for a new parish hall. Perhaps it is because the person feels it is not important to contribute to the salaries of the church staff. It could be that contributing to paying the church utilities does not excite him, but playing a large role in the future of the church does. Whatever the answer, we as Christians must do a better job educating our members as to what it costs to provide the vital ministries in our community on an annual basis. More churches than not would benefit greatly from one consolidated effort to educate and encourage Christian stewardship in their congregations. Therefore, the challenge is to clearly delineate the objectives of each for the congregation.

The real question in deciding a Capital Campaign's timing should be the urgency of your needs, not the timing of the Annual Campaign. Today, nearly half of the projects we are involved in conduct the Annual and Capital Campaign simultaneously. The basic tenets of the campaign strategy remain the same: all the visits are conducted personally and respectfully and educate the congregation on the different goals each campaign supports.

To help make this clear to the congregation, we believe that there should be two different pledge cards, one for Annual Campaign and one for Capital Campaign. The cards should be printed in different colors to further distinguish between the two. When approaching the church member, the request for a pledge must revolve around at least maintaining current annual giving levels while stretching for the longer-term pledge for the capital effort, usually three to five years.

My firm has helped church clients achieve great results using this manner of conducting joint campaigns. Even while requesting church members to simply maintain their current levels of giving to the Annual Campaign, we usually experience a 5 to 10 percent increase (occasionally higher) in total pledges to the Annual Campaign. The reason may be due to two important factors. First, all requests are made in person to church members who are asked to prayerfully consider inspirational giving by their peers. Second, our method involves including all members of the church. Our method of fund raising will always generate a greater number of families participating and pledging to the Annual Campaign. In addition, our Capital Campaigns continue to generate an average of five times annual giving. Although part-time firms will challenge our results (because they cannot achieve them), our clients are more than happy to discuss the success they experienced with our method. Full-time, on-site direction of all aspects of the campaign coupled with a highly ethical approach is our secret to successful campaigns.

> Recently, I went to a meeting at a church at which I did a project several years ago. The pastor stood up and said, "When I last met with Jim, he told me that annual pledges typically do not increase during the pledging period." He then said, "Well, he lied. We saw a 10 percent increase in annual giving during the first year of the campaign."

Here are the advantages and disadvantages of conducting the Annual and Capital Campaigns together that have been reported to me over the years by pastors who have tried to do this with other fund raising consulting firms.

Advantages

1. The campaign is usually conducted in the fall, the traditional time for fund raising. Most people are back to full-time church activity following the vacation season.
2. Those interested in the Annual Campaign will be more apt to support a Capital Campaign.
3. Combining campaigns maximizes the volunteers' time and effort.
4. The membership will become acquainted with a high quality, every-member visitation program that will be of value in future fund raising efforts.

Disadvantages

1. If not done properly, or you do not have a consultant available to monitor both simultaneously, one cause may hurt the other.
2. If not done properly, it is difficult to get any significant increase in the annual pledging during the period of the Capital Campaign.
3. Appraisals may be done for the capital gift pledge but for not the annual budget.

While we enjoy all of the advantages of combining the two campaigns, our method does not experience any of the disadvantages. If a dual campaign is considered to be in the best interest of the client, there are some things that will improve the chances of success and there are some things that should be avoided.

Things to Do

1. Use separate pledge cards—different colors. The annual budget card should be for one year and the Capital Campaign card for three years or more.
2. The case for both elements of the campaign must be very clear and well presented in print and in person.
3. Resist any effort to reduce giving to the annual budget in order to give to the Capital Campaign, or vice versa.
4. Emphasize the proper relationship between the two elements. Generally, the annual budget is basic while the Capital Campaign is "over and above" giving.
5. Have the pastor emphasize the difference between stewardship and fund raising.
6. Develop a comprehensive training program.
7. Gather as much information as possible about current pledges and pledging families.

Things to Avoid

1. Don't allow competition between the goals of the annual budget and the capital needs. The annual budget is necessary to provide for the most vital ministries the church offers.
2. Don't campaign for any significant increase in the annual budget.
3. Don't allow a combined goal with certain percentages to be specified for each of the two elements.

Main Message

The needs of the congregation are more important than trying to "time" the campaign.
Capital Campaigns should never adversely affect Annual Campaigns.

CHAPTER 12

Parting Thoughts

I am often challenged by churches on how my firm, which focuses on the financial aspects of a Stewardship Campaign, can say we are promoting Stewardship and not just fund-raising. My response is very clear, Stewardship is a complex process of engaging the congregation in discussions of current and needed ministries, finding out their interests, educating them about needs of which they are not aware but should be, and encouraging their support with time, talent or treasure. Through the Feasibility Study we engage the congregation and assist in the education of the church. Through the campaign we encourage their inspirational and prayerful generosity.

We are not hired to become spiritual advisors to your church; we leave that to the church leadership. However, through our experience we are prepared to assist churches who are having difficulty finding the right way to present their needs and plans in a spiritual way. Unlike other firms, we allow the church leadership to ask for that help if needed, rather than presume they lack that ability.

There is a growing epidemic among churches throughout the United States. It is an inability or unwillingness to grasp the concept of return on investment with regard to selecting a professional consultant. I see this manifested as a vestry's or church council's inability to see past the showmanship of the sales presenter and focus on the outcome of the project.

A church had an annual giving of $2 million. It needed to raise $6 million. The church hired a part-time firm seven years ago. The firm helped the leaders raise $1.9 million, almost reaching one times annual giving. After the pledging period was over, the church had needs of $10 million, $4 million of which was debt reduction from the last campaign.

For the next campaign, the leaders decided that perhaps they should do something different and interview another consulting firm. They interviewed my firm and the same firm that conducted the last campaign. A few days after the presentation, I was contacted by the pastor and informed that the church was going to give the part-time firm another try, in part due to cost and in part due to their "spiritual" approach to fund raising. I wished the pastor the best of luck and reminded him that any part-time firm was not going to get him the results he needed. This comment always falls on deaf ears, but I feel a moral obligation to say it.

A year later, I followed up, as I always do, and it turned out that the pastor was now gone. The campaign had been a failure, raising only $1.6 million toward the needs of $10 million.

This would be a sad story if it was just one church, but it is a tragedy because it is so many churches that I encounter. When I told this story to my wife, who is a physician, she said, "One of the definitions of insanity is doing the same thing over and over and expecting a different outcome."

Part of what I love best about what I do is getting to be involved with a church that is building and growing. No one enjoys conducting a campaign that's only focus is debt reduction, however sometimes it must be done. Unfortunately, I am being consulted more and more to help salvage churches that were afflicted by an inability to understand that you get the kind of counsel you pay for. Checking references is of utmost importance when making important decisions. We highly encourage anyone, who needs to raise significant funds, to call churches that have gone through the process.

A church that had incurred one million dollars in debt from a failed campaign they had attempted on their own 10 years earlier, contacted me to direct their next campaign. They had done the last campaign on their own in order to save the expense of outside counsel. During my initial meeting, I discussed the fee for directing their campaign. They expressed their reservations over the cost of outside counsel. I explained that retaining a qualified fund raising consultant was an investment, not an expense. I further explained that the annual interest they were paying on their debt was more than our one time fee. In this context, the members of the committee voted unanimously to move forward with my firm.

There are a few overarching points I want everyone to take away from this book.

First, find a fund-raising partner, someone who will serve as a project manager and a coach, someone who will be with you every step of the way. Find someone objective to the needs and vision you have, not someone driven or compensated by a percentage of the funds raised.

Second, don't let anyone tell you what you can or cannot raise. You will read stories of churches that raised ten times or more their annual giving with our method and other churches that could not raise one times annual giving with another method. Every case is different. The leadership of the church and a well-implemented, proven plan are essential to succeed. On that note, let me reiterate that the cause of the campaign (or the Case for Support) can affect the level of giving. You may have the greatest consultant in the world with a great plan, but if the focus of the campaign is to raise money to pay off a debt you acquired from overbuilding and poor planning from the last campaign, it will be a challenge. Even with the best campaign plan, two to three times annual giving would be an accomplishment for a campaign where the sole purpose is debt reduction.

Third, do not start recruiting your campaign committee before selecting your fund-raising consultant, just as you would not hire an electrician to wire your home before you hired the architect to design it.

Fourth, after you hire your consultant, listen to him/her. You are paying for the experience and expertise.

Fifth, there is never a best time to conduct a campaign, but some times are better than others. Do not let the economy or world events affect needs that you identify. If the needs are important to the congregation, the congregation will support them.

Finally, let me say that having a successful campaign is more important than the amount of money raised. When people feel that they are part of something worthwhile and successful, the event will be remembered. Your congregation and its leaders should enjoy the spiritual awakening created when all members of the church work together toward a common goal and provide important ministries to future generations. That being said, don't set a goal that you cannot reach. Listen to your consultant; he/she should advise you to determine a reasonable goal, which you can achieve and surpass.

Please don't attempt a campaign on your own, unless you only have needs of one times annual giving. If that is the case, I hope I have convinced you that with a little effort, you could raise that on your own and you don't need outside counsel.

I wish you great success on your Stewardship journey.

APPENDIX 1

Selected Campaign Prayers

Gracious and loving God,
Fill our hearts with gratitude . . .
For the blessings we have received from those who have walked before us in this church,
For the abundance of gifts and service we offer to You in the ministry of this church,
For this community, with its vibrant joy and hope;
Fill our souls . . . .
With trust in our Savior Jesus Christ who welcomes us to abundant life,
With hope in the Holy Spirit who constantly renews and reconciles the world through
    us,
With joy in the promise of a shared eternity with our God and those we have loved in
    ages past;
Fill our minds with the vision . . . .
That our church may continue to be a tower of light to our county and our city for
    our future,
That we may witness to Christ and serve the needs of our community afresh,
That our Church may be a renewed place of prayer, service, and worship for ages to
    come.
Enable us and inspire us . . .
To do the work that stands before us,
To build a renewed center for ministry, gatherings, education, and service that celebrates
    our love for You,
That we may proclaim Your might, majesty, sovereignty, and power.
This we ask in the name of God: Father, Son, and Holy Spirit.
Amen.

*   *   *

O Gracious and Holy Father, Almighty God, Creator and Protector of this parish church and all who worship here, we bless Thy holy name. We give thanks to Thee for all Thy goodness and favor to this community of Thy faithful people. Look favorably upon us as we acknowledge Thy love by responding to the needs of our neighbors today and tomorrow. Bless our efforts and us as we work for the coming of Thy kingdom by providing to all who worship here a spacious, secure, and accessible place in which to experience Thy love and kindness. Give each of us the courage to share with this and future generations the benefits that we ourselves have received. This we ask in the name of Thy Son, Jesus Christ. Amen

*   *   *

Almighty God, we praise You. We thank You for
the many blessings given us in this good land where
You have blessed us to be a blessing to others.

Grant that Your Holy Spirit will empower us to
provide the just needs of our church and its
mission outreach.

Let us evidence the joy of generosity in our pledge
to our Capital Campaign. We pray this in
the name of Jesus Christ, our Lord. *Amen*

*   *   *

Holy God,
who calls the world into being,
who calls us into Christ's church,
We give thanks for the great heritage of faith
passed down to us from generation to generation.
And we give thanks for this hallowed space of worship and community,
which has been a place of refuge, a seed of courage,
a beacon of light and our true home.
As we embark upon this next journey of faith
grant us the strength of your guiding presence.
By Your grace, transform our gratitude at Your great gifts
into generous discipleship.
May the improvements we seek outwardly
mirror the inward refining of our souls so that

we, like our brothers and sisters who have gone before,
become the church that reflects Your radiance
and works anew to heal a broken world.
Amen

*   *   *

O God of every true renaissance and renewal, always You resist our attempts to define and confine You. At every point, You make us realize that our view is too small, our vision too narrow, and our ideas for our future too limited. Yet for those who attempt to make You in their image, You break loose with newness and surprise.

Now, we come to the point where we, like people in every age past, must merge renewal of vision and commitment with the material-of-the-earth renewal for our ministry center.

As individuals and as a community, in Christ Jesus we have been restored. Just as You make us new, so the time has come when we must restore our church, "our temple" where, through the years, so many have been baptized into faith, heard scriptures proclaimed, and have committed souls back to thee.

As we consider great questions that will guide us into the future, we pray that "the future" which we speak of today, will be "the future" You would have for us.

In the dreams of all Your people, Lord, grant us clear glimpses of You—timeless, mysterious and gracious. Expand our vision. Expand our hope. Expand our love. In the name of Jesus Christ, our guardian, guide, and stay, we invoke Your name.

Amen

*   *   *

O source of strength and power, You call us Your children, and Your love for us is great. You have given us the responsibility of being Your ambassadors, inviting others to know and love You. Help us to be faithful to our task. Dear God of miracles, as we set out to care for the building with which You have entrusted us and to expand our ministries and facilities, please enable us to accomplish our goals. Bring forth from us the energy and the wisdom and the resources necessary. Guide all that lead our campaign, and bless our church. In Christ's name we pray. Amen

*   *   *

Gracious and loving God,
Our hearts are filled with gratitude . . .
for the blessings we have received from those that have walked before us in this
    church
for this church family and its abundance of talents and service so freely shared for Your
    glory

Our souls are filled with hope . . .
That our church be a house of worship for all people, an entrance that will welcome
    all that come
this way, and a space of gathering for our community
hat the improvements we seek outwardly inspire us to grow in areas of service that we
    have not even imagined
Our minds are filled with the vision . . .
that instills in us the will and the courage to move forward in faith
that creates excitement and momentum, passion for the goal, and compassion for those
    around us for Your glory
Enable and inspire us . . .
to remember the past with thankfulness
continue our journey to You with eagerness and with renewed commitment
and realize our dreams
Amen

*   *   *

O Gracious and Faithful Lord,
You have called us to build our house upon the rock. Like Your disciple Peter,
that rock is our faith in Your Son given to us through Your Holy Spirit. We thank
You for nurturing in us this gift of faith. We pray that You would continue to
nurture and grow that faith in us that we may become ever more trusting in Your
abundant grace so freely given. May Your lamp be the light to lead us as we work
to build Your kingdom here in our community. Give us courage to share Your
Good News in word and deed. Grow in us faithful giving hearts. May our efforts
serve to glorify You, the Almighty One, in the name of the Father, and the Son
and the Holy Spirit,
Amen

*   *   *

APPENDIX 2

Letters to Congregations

Dear members,

In 1931, our predecessor members of this congregation established a magnificent gothic structure at this location to be their new home. They also accepted the honor, and responsibility of being designated the National Church of Methodism.

They and their successors, including some still among us, subsequently grew the facility in two stages, one in 1957 and the other, familiar to most of us, in 2000. Growth not due to an edifice complex, but to better accommodate the vibrant and diverse ministries centered here—work of our Lord in teaching, preaching and serving our community and beyond. From Presidents to the homeless—all have been welcomed and nourished in these spaces.

We are now called to act to ensure that this facility can continue, in the 21st century, to be as vibrant and useful to the faithful and needy as it was in the 20th. A calling by which we become a bridge between our faithful and generous predecessors and our children and others who will find a home here for decades to come.
Our needs are in three parts:

First, to restore the basic structure, including the stained glass windows, to its proper form and integrity.

Second, to enhance the outside appearance to make our site more visible, functional, and enticing to those who would see us for the first time—and helpful to all of us as we spend our time and talents here.

Third, to enhance the interior of our church in terms of its appearance and functionality. To transform it from a worn and tired looking place to one that shines and up-lifts as we look upon it and/or use it for our worship and programs.

These needs were tested in the Focus Group Meetings conducted July 11th-August 15th. We were delighted that during 16 focus groups, over 300 members of the congregation attending with almost universal agreement that we need to act immediately. Following the very positive feedback from those meetings, a church conference was held in order to officially determine the will of our congregation. As you are all probably aware, a *unanimous* vote to proceed with a Capital Campaign occurred. This is the foundation required for a successful campaign effort.

I am honored and humbled to have been selected to lead this campaign effort. A dedicated team of individuals has been assembled to work tirelessly to achieve our goal of giving every member of our church the opportunity to share in this vital and worthy project.

Guiding and conducting a campaign will involve many members of the congregation and staff—all who will be volunteering to do what they would probably not elect to do if there were a choice. But they are volunteering because they know there is no acceptable choice other than doing all we can to meet our historic and contemporary responsibilities as stewards and users of this place.

All members of the congregation will be visited by one or more volunteers who will explain further the plans and opportunities and solicit a gift commitment. To those who will be making calls and visits, my heartfelt thanks. To all members of the congregation my thanks for being open to the call and visit, and to considering an inspirational gift toward our need.

The campaign is scheduled to be completed by the end of this year. We are currently developing campaign materials and recruiting campaign volunteers. Our campaign kickoff event is scheduled for October 27 and will be the official beginning of our effort with a congregational dinner. You will soon be getting a personal invitation to this event. I encourage all of you to make every effort to attend what is sure to be a terrific and memorable evening.

I want to that you in advance for your prayerful consideration on how you can join us in this opportunity for our church to refurbish, refresh, and re-energize for the Lord's work. I thank you and the generations that follow us will surely thank you.

Frank Trotter
Metropolitan Memorial UMC

*   *   *

Dear Friends,

There are times in our lives that what we do changes everything for us . . . and for all who come after us. 1952 was such a time when St. Mark's was founded out of three Methodist town churches and made the decision to build a new church on this site. Now, it is our time.

"Growing to Serve" is about making a very fine facility more available to more people.

The Lord's work is always done through the generosity of His people, because we know of the generosity of Christ's sacrifice of love on the cross. It took incredible generosity and faith in 1952 to create a new church-center of God honoring community ministry.

Yes, this new task that we are facing is monumental. It is a 1-in-50 year endeavor. Yet, our call—to go into all the world with the Gospel—is huge! To obey God's call, there are times when we must undertake monumental tasks.

Take time to consider this call. We know what we say about the generation that created St. Mark's. What will people say about us 50 years from now? Only you and I hold the answer.

Thank you for your generosity and love of St. Mark's!

I am:

Faithfully yours in Christ,

Gary L. Moore
Senior Pastor

*   *   *

My Dear Parishioners and Friends of St. Paul's,

You and I are the benefactors of the legacy of those who came before us at St. Paul's, clergy and laity alike. For example Pillsbury House, which presently houses much of our formation and fellowship space, was a gift to our parish in 1957. Because of that wonderful gift, we have enjoyed the use of a building that has served us well for three generations.

In 1945, our congregation faced the challenge of enforced removal from our original cite on Washington Circle and took the bold step to build on the present site. Surely it was the hope of those who built our lovely church that one day a future congregation would take another bold step and ensure its completion.

While the Catholic Faith remains timeless, the needs and demands of active congregations necessarily change. Life expectancies and the expectations of parishioners have changed and grown. The inadequacies and weaknesses of an aging plant become more and more obvious with the passing years.

The calendar itself gives us a significant moment in history as we evoke a new millennium. American society has also rarely seen such economic prosperity, despite the social challenge of which we are only too aware in this city. The time is ripe for us to do something monumental and *The Millennium Fund* at St. Paul's provides us all with that opportunity.

First, our gifts to this fund at this significant time in history will record our thanks for our many blessings past and present. Our gifts will also give us the opportunity to acknowledge immediate needs clearly outlined in this brochure—and to be faithful to those, perhaps none of whom we shall ever see, but those who will succeed us here for generations to come.

I hope that you will join me in seizing this opportunity by generous and spiritual giving to *The Millennium Fund* at St. Paul's. May our gifts be sacrificial signs of our thankfulness for the past and our faithfulness to the future.

Yours In Christ,
Andrew L. Sloane

*   *   *

Dear Church Members,

One hundred and fifty years ago the members of Evangelical Lutheran Church took a bold step in faith as they entered into a building program to construct our majestic twin spires on Church Street. Their desire to glorify God left an indelible mark on the history of our church family and has literally blessed thousands and thousands of souls since that time. When I think of their faith and sacrifice to bless people like me—people they would never know this side of heaven—I am humbled.

Since returning from service in Iraq I have been amazed to witness how the Holy Spirit has been moving among the people of Evangelical Lutheran Church in the eight months that I've been away. Visions of who we believe God wants us to be in our complex and ever changing world have been articulated in the final envisioning task force report. The congregation, in its March 2005 meeting joyfully adopted this vision and work commenced for a Capital Campaign to provide the platform to enable these ministries to happen. We have taken careful steps to assess our readiness—asking if we were in keeping with the Lord's timing.

Now we stand together, much like our forebearers did 150 years ago—prepared to embark on a journey. It is a journey marked by faith and sacrifice. I honestly believe that it's a journey that will not only bless us in the near future but it will also enrich the lives of countless people we will never know this side of heaven.

Together we will care for the children of Evangelical Lutheran Church and the community through a renovation of our Schaeffer Center in Frederick. Together we will purchase land in Urbana and create worship space through modifications of an existing building on that land. These efforts will shape the communities of southern Frederick county for Christ's purposes. Together we will secure adjacent properties in Frederick to enable our ministry to the community to grow. Together our faith and sacrifice will bless thousands and thousands of souls in the years to come.

To be very honest, the challenge before us is a big one. However, I believe that the resources to fund these identified needs are within our reach. I am also convinced, that like our forebearers in faith, we are a people completely committed to glorifying God as we return thanks for His countless blessings in our lives.

The underlying strength that makes all of this possible is our deep faith in God made known to us in Jesus Christ. It is this faith that unites and strengthens us for discipleship in Christ's name. It is this faith that brings to mind the words of scripture that remind us that "with God, all things are possible!"

Thank you for what you will decide to do now to help continue the mission and ministry of this great church. May God's strength and power be with us as we move forward to His glory.

In Christ's Service,
The Rev. Dr. David G. Oravec, Senior Pastor

*   *   *

Dear church members,

We read in scripture that longevity is a gift from God. We certainly have received this gift. We have been blessed with 125 years of receiving Jesus in the Eucharist and praising God in His Holy Temple. Over the course of those years, we have responded to growth of the Catholic population by establishing a parish for the University Community, one for the Afro-American Community and another for those living north of Charlottesville.

Holy Comforter was also the catalyst for the Catholic School, affordable housing and outreach to the poor. I recommend that you study our history presented in this book to understand who we are as the Church of the Holy Comforter.

Doing the work of the Lord is like breathing. You have to inhale and exhale. We have exhaled generosity through our ministries and personal commitment to our Church. It is time to inhale lest we run out of breath. We need to create space so that a variety of ministries and services that will nurture us can be provided. We need to create space for our youth and teens to gather during the week. We need to create space so that inter-faith activities can be sponsored by us. We need to create space to be able to respond to new ideas and needs that are yet to be defined.

I am asking everyone to step forward as you have done over and over and wholeheartedly support our Capital Campaign. We are calling it Love in Action. Let us pray that throughout our Campaign, God will bless everyone with the fruit of their generosity.

In the Risen Lord,
Father Dennis McAuliffe

*   *   *

Dear Members and Friends of First Presbyterian Church,

What a privilege it is to pastor this fine congregation. Though I have only been here a year and a half, your welcome and enthusiasm have made me quickly feel at home. Our worship attendance is up. New programs are beginning, new staff is on board. We had an excellent stewardship campaign last fall, and have reached new levels in our support for ministry, mission, and worship.

Now I write to you with a important opportunity. The Session of the church has approved a Capital Campaign in order to make much needed repairs to our facility. We have also committed ourselves to finding the resources to help promote Christ's mission in the larger community. Our *"Faith in Action"* campaign will seek pledges from you in order to make our church building (which is now fifty years old) completely ready for the next fifty years of ministry. This campaign will also enable us to support Christian ministry through groups like Habitat for Humanity, Daughters of Zelophehad, Union Seminary, a medical clinic for children in Nicaragua, and more.

This is an opportunity for us to practice the joy of generosity. We have been blessed so that we may be a blessing to others. We have been called together as a church family so that we may serve in the "family business" of caring about each other and all God's children. We have the ability and the privilege of giving as a way to put our faith into action, and our hope into help for this congregation and many other people. Please carefully read the material about our goals for the *"Faith in Action"* Capital Campaign. When one of your fellow members calls on you for your pledge, please make a gift that is both joyful and sacrificial. Let it be joyful to show our gratitude for all that God has done for us. Let it be sacrificial to show our deep commitment to making God's love real in the world today.

Thank you for making this effort a success, and for starting this new century off as faithful and generous people of God. I am

Yours in Christ,
Rev. Charlie Summers

*   *   *

Dear Members of the Faith Lutheran Family:

It is with great pride and excitement that I write to you about the fundraising drive for our new fellowship hall. Our congregation has been growing and as we add new programs and services for parishioners of all ages, we face a pressing need to expand our facilities. I am honored to have the opportunity to be your pastor during this critical stage of the church's development, and I look forward to working with all of you to move us through this momentous transition.

For four years we have been planning for this new addition to our facility. We've worked closely with an architect, visited other churches to inspire our dreams and, most importantly, invited all of you to share your hopes and concerns with us so that we could develop a place of worship and fellowship that truly meets the needs of the congregation.

In addition to our new facility, which is described in detail on the following pages, 10 percent of the funds raised through this campaign will support the Haiti Lazarus Project, Lutheran Outdoor Ministries, and Lutheran Social Services of Florida.

God has graced us with an amazing opportunity to serve the needs of our members and our community more fully. Since I came to this church as an associate pastor in 1986, I have felt the warmth, humanity and generosity of our parishioners. I ask you now to listen closely to your neighbor as they explain the goals of this campaign to you and do all that you can to help us build our future in faith.

I hope that you will join with me and our church leaders, all of whom have made personal commitments to make this project succeed, in making this inspiring vision for our future a reality.

Your servant in Christ,
Pastor Steve

*   *   *

Dear Members of St. Paul's,

Thank you for prayerfully considering a leadership gift to our "Building for Innovation" Capital Campaign. As you contemplate your participation in this compelling project, I invite you to reflect on the unique role a Christian congregation plays in God's plan of salvation.

The congregation is God's chief means by which the Holy Spirit converts and sanctifies us, empowers us to be Christ's emissaries in the world, and prepares us for fuller life with God in heaven. Put differently, a congregation is about experiencing God's forgiveness through Jesus; it is about changing self-absorbed lives into self-giving lives; it is about our becoming more Christ-like by using the means God gives us to grow into maturity (inspirational worship, Bible study, loving relationships, serving the wider community, to name just a few); the congregation is about the salvation of souls. Accordingly, in my opinion, there is no more important enterprise worthy of the Christian's support.

Giving to this renovation/expansion project is a tangible way for us to thank God for the many ways God has shaped us and made us who we are because of the Holy Spirit's unique presence in our congregation. More than that, we give thanks not just for how St. Paul's has mediated Jesus' salvation to us but for how it has done so for countless others in the past, in the present, and in the future. The bold plan to expand the church, replace our failing pipe organ, develop the property between our two buildings (formerly 61st street), build a new Parish Hall, and renovate the Parish Center to provide better space for our children and youth, is a concrete way by which we can glorify God and create buildings and a campus-like setting that will continue to draw people into relationship with our Lord for decades to come.

My wife, Margie, and I are supporting this project with our resources because we believe in the exciting future God has in store for St. Paul's. We have pledged to this campaign because we are thankful for the Holy Spirit's transforming presence in this congregation.

God be with you as you consider your gift.

Faithfully yours in Christ,
Richard H. Winters

APPENDIX 3

Testimonials from Clients

When we realized that it was time to step back and analyze many of the long-term maintenance needs of the church, we decided to conduct a feasibility study to ensure that all members were engaged in the process and that all issues were addressed. We were fortunate to have had the counsel of James D. Klote & Associates to guide us through this process. We found that many members of the congregation felt as strongly about mission and outreach as they did in taking care of our own needs. Therefore, our campaign was tailored to encourage the congregation's equal support of those two goals. We challenged ourselves to raise $1.5 million for deferred maintenance and $1.5 million for mission and outreach.

With the help of our full-time consultant, we were able to surpass the $3 million dollar mark! Our consultant was not only very knowledgeable and professional; his commitment to the life of the church was obvious from the start. I can not overemphasize the blessing it was to have someone else responsible to set up the campaign calendar, prepare the rooms for meetings, and keep us all on track so that we could continue to perform our daily responsibilities. He met weekly with the steering committee, gave training to our visitors, kept all the campaign records, and helped us make key decisions as the campaign progressed. His experience and temperament were just the right fit for First Presbyterian.

I recommend without reservation James D. Klote & Associates, this plan of campaign, and the benefits of full-time consultation.

Rev. Charles A. Summers, Pastor
First Presbyterian Church
Richmond, Virginia

*   *   *

After an extensive national search, I can say with great confidence that we chose the very best! I want you to know how pleased I am that St. Paul's retained JDK&A as our capital campaign counsel. Our resident consultant was with us for a five-month period. During that time he oversaw a feasibility study and helped direct the advanced gifts phase of our campaign so that at our parish-wide kick-off event we were able to announce that we had already received $6.5 million in pledges, which represents 10 times annual giving. Your firm gave our campaign volunteers the training and confidence we needed for completing all of our visits.

> The Rev. Richard H. Winters
> St. Paul's Episcopal Church
> Indianapolis, Indiana

*   *   *

The capital stewardship firm of James D. Klote & Associates provided us with the best possible support for our new building campaign. Our on-site Director did an outstanding job of motivating us and keeping us on track to ensure a great campaign victory. He provided the direction to assist us in completing the necessary tasks so crucial in a successful effort. We would highly recommend JDK&A to any church considering a capital stewardship campaign. Our Campaign Committee unanimously agreed that we could not have raised the amount we did without your help!

> Rev. Russell B. McClatchey
> Mt. Harmony United Methodist Church
> Owings, Maryland

*   *   *

James D. Klote & Associates has provided our Catholic Community with a proven process, tailored to our specific needs and circumstance. The advice, dedicated effort, and wholehearted commitment to our campaign has been singularly outstanding. Our consultant, who directed our "Love In Action" Campaign, is a true professional. He is an ethical, organized and tireless executive who has been relentless in the pursuit of our campaign goals. The benefits of having a JDK&A Campaign Director on-site are incalculable It has been a pleasure to work with him and other JDK&A staff members. I strongly commend James D. Klote and Associates to any organization seeking success in their philanthropic financial endeavors.

> Mr. James Neale, Campaign Chair
> Holy Comforter Catholic Church
> Charlottesville, Virginia

*   *   *

Our Director from JDK&A walked us through the process of inviting the parish family to help us give shape to the vision during our time of listening in focus group meetings. The clear, but kind direction he exerted during the pledge drive enabled us to achieve what we once thought was an impossible goal. JDK&A understands churches, the process of arriving at a common vision and was engaged in making this campaign a success. We have passed our goal of $4,750,000 and now have a pledge base of over $5,000,000, which is 6 times annual giving! We have been drawn closer as a parish family through this whole process.

Dr. Peter B. Stube
Christ Episcopal Church
New Bern, North Carolina

*   *   *

The whole Klote organization is trustworthy and utilized techniques that are of the utmost ethical benchmarks. For Faith Lutheran Church, Sarasota, our fundraising has been seen as a ministry, and James D. Klote and Associates offered the professionalism and expertise to be our true partners in this ministry. They have invested themselves in our campaign in every way, blessing our parishioners with their joyful presence. Gracious enthusiasm coupled with time tested methods made our campaign a success even before we began. I wholeheartedly recommend them as a fundraising firm without peer.

Rev. Stephen P. Winemiller
Faith Lutheran Church
Sarasota, Florida

*   *   *

I thank James D. Klote & Associates for their guidance, hard work, positive attitude and friendship. The JDK&A professionals provided invaluable assistance in preparing and implementing a thorough Feasibility Study. This allowed all members of our church an opportunity to advise and accept ownership in our new building plans. The Study helped focus our intentions and gather the support needed to proceed with an immensely successful fund raising campaign.

Rev. Jack Ewald, Pastor
Potomac United Methodist Church
Potomac, Maryland

*   *   *

Having a full-time consultant on campus was extremely helpful as we dealt with the nuts and bolts of the campaign. The level of confidence increased with each visit due to good training and by providing the necessary position descriptions in regards to what needed to be done. Thank you for the materials and guidance you provided. I would look to James D. Klote & Associates again for a campaign.

> Rev. Dr. Edward K. Brandt
> Red Clay Creek Presbyterian Church
> Wilmington, Delaware

*   *   *

One of the reasons we hired your firm was your promise to be with us and lead us every step of the way. Our Director did just that and gave his personal attention to the details as well. The campaign has gone very smoothly so far, and I am confident that more than enough money will be raised to do everything that we have planned. I appreciate the fact that you emphasized the importance of relating the campaign to our mission. This will enable us to grow and expand our ministries for years to come.

> The Rev. Danny Schieffler
> St. John's Episcopal Church
> Fort Smith, Arkansas

*   *   *

When we first had the pleasure of meeting and discussing the elements necessary for a successful fund raising campaign, we agree that in order to be true to our faith, we must treat all families, within our church family, in the same manner. You helped us make that goal a reality. In doing so, our church community has been strengthened. It is incredible what can be achieved when we all work together toward a common goal."

> Rev. G. Robert Hottinger
> Glenelg United Methodist Church
> Glenelg, Maryland

*   *   *

Gateway Trinity Lutheran Church recently conducted a Capital Stewardship Program to reduce long-term indebtedness, which began to negatively affect our mission and ministries. By involving the total congregation in a Readiness Assessment, we were able to fully explain our current needs and our opportunities. Through this process of engaging our church family, we enjoyed an outstanding campaign success. Our church now has a firm financial foundation in which to build as we consider new ministry opportunities in Fort Myers. We benefited considerably from the full-time, personalized approach of James D. Klote & Associates.

> Rev. Kent R. Lee
> Gateway Trinity Lutheran Church
> Ft. Myers, Florida

*　　*　　*

"Through the assistance of JDK&A we are experiencing the most successful fundraising campaign in the history of our parish. The professional full-time consulting services of James D. Klote & Associates has proven to be invaluable to our "Shine As a Light" capital campaign

> The Rev. Oran Warder
> St. Paul's Episcopal Church
> Alexandria, Virginia

*　　*　　*

The full-time resident services of JDK&A helped us raise more money than in any other campaign in the history of ELC . . . $2,533,000! As a Business Administrator, I highly support and recommend this firm to any church considering a capital campaign.

> Mr. Chuck Huber
> Church Business Administrator
> Evangelical Lutheran Church
> Frederick, Maryland

*　　*　　*

We simply could not have done this on our own. One challenge of the campaign was how to approach the parish on the heels of a recent campaign and the delicacies involved in a new approach to parishioners who already gave sacrificially. We were certain that we needed the on-site and intensive presence of JDK&A consultant. Without exception, our leadership would recommend your firm, your philosophy, and your work to anyone. It would be difficult to imagine any better in the business.

> The Rev. Andrew L. Sloane, Rector
> St. Paul's Parish
> Washington, DC

*   *   *

Your Consultant provided excellent guidance and resources to the Capital Campaign. He led us through the process step by step with written materials to further clarify. He was present at the weekly Campaign Steering Committee meeting and helped each member of the committee understand and carry out his/her individual responsibilities. The full time service offered by your firm was extremely helpful and beneficial. We exceeded our goal and completed our work in the allotted time frame.

> The Rev. Cheryl Ann Winter
> St. Timothy-in-the-Valley Episcopal Church
> Hurricane, West Virginia

*   *   *

I speak for our church leaders when I say I can't imagine conducting a capital campaign-no matter what the goal-any other way. James D. Klote & Associates full-time, on-site presence made all the difference! Our consultant was available, accessible and eager to guide at every point along the way—for steering committee meetings, training sessions, home visits, maintaining records and producing reports. Our experience bears witness that, given their unique approach, it is no surprise that JDK&A achieve a higher level of success than competing firms.

> Rev. E. Taveirne, Senior Pastor
> Gary United Methodist Church
> Wheaton, Illinois

*   *   *

I write to express my pleasure with James D. Klote & Associates in our Sharing God's Gifts Capital Campaign. In particular I commend the efforts of your consultant who worked tirelessly. His continual presence and experience helped St. David's accomplish what has never been accomplished before in raising funds for our present and future capital needs.

Your consultant not only performed his responsibilities in the most complete and professional manner, but he became one of us at St. David's for which we are grateful. He took great care with our volunteers, our Campaign visitors and Steering Committee.

Such commitment speaks well not only of him as your associate but also as one who loves and is devoted to his calling. Thank you for recommending him to us.

We at St. David's look forward to a continuing relationship with James D. Klote & Associates as we seek to share God's gifts with one another and our community.

The Rev. Gary Rowe
St. David's Episcopal Church
Wilmington, Delaware

*   *   *

There is something to be said for persistence!

In 1997 an archdiocesan review told us that Saint Matthew could raise between $200,000 and $314,000. We desperately needed much more than that. We sought out a professional consulting firm that would help us achieve our needs. We chose James D. Klote & Associates who sent us a consultant who helped us raise $1,892,000!

Recently, the congregation realized we needed a parish hall, however, not all of the pledges from the last campaign had been collected. We desperately needed a solution. We called again on James D. Klote & Associates who sent us the consultant who led us to victory in our first campaign. He helped us to design a campaign that merged the two appeals in a seamless and sensible manner.

The parishioners responded to the plan and the call and once again we reached our goal. There is something to be said for persistence and having confidence in your consultant. That is easy to do with one as professional, effective and able to tailor a campaign for your needs, as was our consultant.

St. Matthew will rely on James D. Klote & Associates for any and all future fund raising needs.

Father Jose Ortega
St. Matthew Catholic Church
Hillsboro, Oregon

*   *   *

If you don't want the day-to-day campaign work to fall on you or your staff, I would encourage you to give JDK&A an opportunity to see what they can do. We are closing in on the $15,000,000 mark, which is close to 9 times our annual giving!!

> Mr. David Kramer
> Church Business Administrator
> First Presbyterian Church
> Ft. Lauderdale, Florida

* * *

Full-time consulting has put us far ahead of what all the other consultants said we could raise. From the moment our on-site consultant appeared, hope grew and expertise abounded. Not only was our consultant well trained, he also became a part of our parish family and a visible encouragement to us all. My daily meetings with him proved to me that we were in good hands as he led us through this process of giving every member an opportunity to be a part of this project.

> The Rev. William J. Bradbury
> St. Peter's Episcopal Church
> Washington, North Carolina

* * *

I would like to extend my personal and deep thanks to you for the truly exception job that James D. Klote & Associates performed for Metropolitan Memorial United Methodist Church's Capital Campaign. Our decision to hire you as our campaign consultant was based on several factors—your comprehensive understanding of our church's needs; your track record that churches using your system would produce pledges totaling five times a church's annual giving; your positive references from other churches in our area; your personal warmth, integrity and charm; and your commitment as a Christian to the work that you are doing. Our pledge total has already surpassed six times our annual giving . . . and is continuing to grow.

We are enormously pleased by everything that JDK&A provided for us. Your staff is outstanding. Should Metropolitan Memorial choose to conduct another capital campaign in the future while I am the Senior Pastor, your firm will undoubtedly be at the top of our list.

Thank you, again, for all that you have done for us.

> Rev. Dr. Frank Trotter, Jr
> Metropolitan Memorial United Methodist Church
> Washington, DC

*   *   *

Your firm's leadership for our campaign enabled us to involve and include everyone in our parish. This campaign did much more for our parish family than simply attain a fundraising goal that will provide for expanded facilities. During the campaign, people reconnected with each other and also in their own faith. None of this would have been possible without the assistance and guidance from your firm. I would be most pleased to encourage anyone considering a capital campaign to be in touch with you and your professional colleagues.

> The Rev. Charles E. B. Gill, Rector
> St. Andrew's By-The-Sea Episcopal Church
> Nags Head, North Carolina

*   *   *

Holy Cross Parish, in the Diocese of Atlanta, faced the need to renovate and update our worship space and offices. The Vestry realized we needed more money than was ever raised at a single time in our 46 year history. We further knew that we would require expert counsel. In the process of interviewing fund raising firms, we were fortunate to find James D. Klote & Associates. The skill, enthusiasm and dedication of this firm was the key to the success of our "Lift High the Cross" capital campaign.

With their consultant entering into our community as a full-time parishioner, the campaign took on the feel of a consolidated parish effort. Working together, we surpassed our goal by over 20%! We could not be happier with the results of the campaign and the professionals of James D. Klote & Associates.

When the need arises in the future, I will not hesitate to contact the professionals at James D. Klote & Associates to help my parish continue our mission and ministry of Jesus Christ.

> The Rev. Kent Belmore, Rector
> Holy Cross Parish
> Decatur, Georgia

*   *   *

St. Mark's United Methodist Church raised $2,400,000, thanks to the fundraising consulting firm of James D. Klote & Associates. Compared to what we would have paid for a part-time consultant, the investment in the resident directed service JDK&A offered was inexpensive. We needed a resident consultant to keep us focused and on track throughout the campaign effort. Without full-time consulting, I am convinced we would never have achieved the success we did.

> Rev. Gary L. Moore
> St. Mark's United Methodist Church
> Easton, Maryland

*   *   *

James D. Klote & Associates holds my respect, gratitude, and highest recommendation! When Evangelical Lutheran Church decided to move forward with a capital campaign to create a satellite campus and provide needed improvements to our existing campus, a thorough search of available firms was conducted. James D. Klote and Associates was selected because of their competence, care, track record, and "hands on" approach. As the campaign has unfolded, they have consistently provided a quality of service that has made this a joyful experience.

> Rev. Dave Oravec
> Evangelical Lutheran Church
> Frederick, Maryland

*   *   *

The full-time consulting of JDK&A was the vital component to the success we enjoyed at Gary Memorial United Methodist Church. As a result, we raised $5,800,000, which is 8 times our annual giving!

> Mr. David Brewer
> Church Business Administrator
> Gary Memorial United Methodist Church
> Wheaton, Illinois

*   *   *

James D. Klote & Associates has gone far beyond our expectations in the quality of their service, their attention to detail and their personal interest in who we are as a congregation. We met our goal of $4,000,000 with the help of our JDK&A Director, 5.6 times our annual giving!

> The Rev. James W.H. Sell, Rector
> Christ & St. Luke's Episcopal Church
> Norfolk, Virginia

APPENDIX 4

Bible Quotes on Stewardship

(From the New International Version)

"What good is it, my brothers, if a man claims to have faith but has no deeds? Can such faith save him? Suppose a brother or sister is without clothes and daily food. If one of you says to him, 'Go, I wish you well; keep warm and well fed,' but does nothing about his physical needs, what good is it? In the same way, faith by itself, if it is not accompanied by action, is dead."

James 2:14-17

* * *

"[F]or God loves a cheerful giver."

2 Corinthians 9:7

* * *

"This is how we know what love is: Jesus Christ laid down his life for us. And we ought to lay down our lives for our brothers. If anyone has material possessions and sees his brother in need but has no pity on him, how can the love of God be in him? Dear children, let us not love with words or tongue but with actions and in truth."

1 John 3:16-18

*   *   *

"But just as you excel in everything—in faith, in speech, in knowledge, in complete earnestness and in your love for us—see that you also excel in this grace of giving."

2 Corinthians 8:7

*   *   *

"Jesus looked at him and loved him. 'One thing you lack,' he said. 'Go, sell everything you have and give to the poor, and you will have treasure in heaven. Then come, follow me.'"

Mark 10:21

*   *   *

"Whoever loves money never has money enough; whoever loves wealth is never satisfied with his income. This too is meaningless . . . I have seen a grievous evil under the sun: wealth hoarded to the harm of its owner, or wealth lost through some misfortune, so that when he has a son there is nothing left for him."

Ecclesiastes 5:10, 13-14

*   *   *

"Give, and it will be given to you. A good measure, pressed down, shaken together and running over, will be poured into your lap. For with the measure you use, it will be measured to you."

Luke 6:38

*   *   *

"Calling his disciples to him, Jesus said, 'I tell you the truth, this poor widow has put more into the treasury than all the others. They all gave out of their wealth; but she, out of her poverty, put in everything—all she had to live on.'"

Mark 12:43-44

*   *   *

"'Bring the whole tithe into the storehouse, that there may be food in my house. Test me in this,' says the Lord Almighty, 'and see if I will not throw open the floodgates of heaven and pour out so much blessing that you will not have room enough for it.'"

Malachi 3:10

*   *   *